Microsoft

Microsoft® Official Academic Course: Managing and Maintaining a Microsoft Windows Server™ 2003 Environment for an MCSE Certified on Windows® 2000 (70-296)

Lab Manual

D1456418

Owen Fowler

PUBLISHED BY
Microsoft Press
A Division of Microsoft Corporation
One Microsoft Way
Redmond, Washington 98052-6399

Printed and bound in the United States of America.

1 2 3 4 5 6 7 8 9   QWT   9 8 7 6 5 4

Distributed in Canada by H.B. Fenn and Company Ltd.

A CIP catalogue record for this book is available from the British Library.

Microsoft Press books are available through booksellers and distributors worldwide. For further information about
international editions, contact your local Microsoft Corporation office or contact Microsoft Press International directly at fax
(425) 936-7329. Visit our Web site at www.microsoft.com/learning/. Send comments to *moac@microsoft.com*.

Acquisitions Editor: Linda Engelman
Project Editor: Lynn Finnel
Technical Editor: Kurt Hudson
Copy Editor: Christina Palaia

SubAssy Part No. X10-84324
Body Part No. X10-84326

TABLE OF CONTENTS

LAB 1

REVIEWING MICROSOFT ACTIVE DIRECTORY CONCEPTS

This lab contains the following exercises and activities:

- Exercise 1-1: Installing Active Directory Using the Active Directory Installation Wizard

- Exercise 1-2: Installing Active Directory Using an Answer File

- Exercise 1-3: Raising the Domain Functional Level

- Exercise 1-4: Raising the Forest Functional Level

- Exercise 1-5: Configuring a Global Catalog Server

- Exercise 1-6: Configuring Universal Group Caching

- Lab Review Questions

- Lab Challenge 1-1: Creating Answer Files for Active Directory Installations

SCENARIO

You are a domain enterprise administrator at Contoso, Ltd., an insurance company. Contoso is going to migrate all of its servers to Windows Server 2003. Before doing so, however, they have elected to create a test network and domain to make sure that everything works before deployment. You have been assigned the task of creating this domain.

After completing this lab, you will be able to:

- Create domain controllers using the Active Directory Installation Wizard and using an answer file
- Raise the domain and forest functional levels
- Assign the global catalog server role and configure universal group caching

Estimated completion time: 90 minutes

BEFORE YOU BEGIN

To complete this lab, you'll need to pair with another student so that there is an even-numbered and an odd-numbered computer, according to the computer name, in each pair. It is necessary that the numbers in each pair be consecutive, and recommended that your partner be near you.

This lab often refers to the number of your domain, your computer, or your partner's computer according to the following conventions:

- *xx* is the number of your domain.
- *yy* is the number of your computer.
- *zz* is the number of your partner's computer.

  For example, if you are using Computer04, *xx* = 03 (you are a member of Contoso03.local), *yy* = 04 (you are using Computer04), and *zz* = 03 (your partner is using Computer03).

Copying Lab Folders and Files to your Computer

Estimated completion time: 5 minutes

In this exercise, you will copy files for use in the labs from your Student CD to the root of the C drive on your computer.

1. Log on with your Administrator account. The password is P@ssw0rd.

   NOTE *The 0 character in the password is a zero.*

2. From My Computer or Windows Explorer, open your Student CD. Select the Lab Manual folder at the root of the CD and press CTRL+C to copy the folder.

3. Browse to the root of your C drive. From the Edit menu, select Paste, or press CTRL+V.

EXERCISE 1-1: INSTALLING ACTIVE DIRECTORY USING THE ACTIVE DIRECTORY INSTALLATION WIZARD

Estimated completion time: 25 minutes

To begin creating the test domain, you first need to promote a system to a domain controller. The following exercise will create a new domain within a new forest using the Active Directory Installation Wizard, by promoting your server to a domain controller.

> **IMPORTANT**   Complete this exercise on the odd-numbered computer. The even-numbered computer will be promoted to a replica domain controller in the next exercise.

1. Log on with your Administrator account (the password is P@ssw0rd).

   > **NOTE**   The 0 character in the password is a zero.

2. From the Start menu, select Run.

   > **NOTE**   If your Windows Server 2003 installation CD is not in your CD/DVD drive, you should insert it now. Click Exit if the Welcome To Microsoft Windows Server 2003 screen pops up after you insert the CD.

3. In the Run dialog box, in the Open text box, type **dcpromo** and press ENTER.

4. In the Active Directory Installation Wizard, on the Welcome To The Active Directory Installation Wizard page, click Next.

5. On the Operating System Compatibility page, click Next.

6. On the Domain Controller Type page, verify that Domain Controller For A New Domain is selected, as shown in the following figure. Click Next.

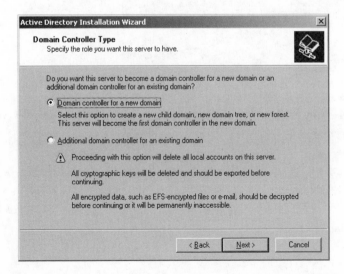

7. On the Create New Domain page, ensure that Domain In A New Forest is selected, and then click Next.

8. On the New Domain Name page, in the Full DNS Name For New Domain text box, type **Contosoyy.local** (for example, Computer03 will have a domain name of Contoso03.local, which will also be the domain that the even-numbered computer is added to in the next exercise). Click Next.

9. On the NetBIOS Domain Name page, the Active Directory Installation Wizard will suggest a NetBIOS name. Accept the default name provided by clicking Next.

10. On the Database And Log Folders page, click Next.

11. On the Shared System Volume page, leave the default location of the Sysvol folder in the Folder Location text box. The SYSVOL folder must reside on a partition or volume formatted with the NTFS file system. Click Next.

12. On the DNS Registration Diagnostics page, verify that the Install And Configure The DNS Server On This Computer, And Set This Computer To Use This DNS Server As Its Preferred DNS Server option is selected, as shown in the following example, and click Next.

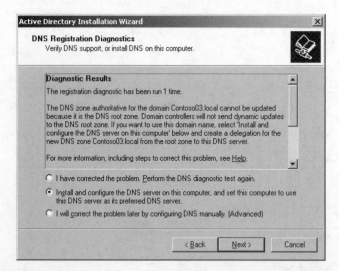

QUESTION   Why is the Active Directory Installation Wizard concerned about DNS?

13. On the Permissions page, accept the default as shown in the following example, and click Next.

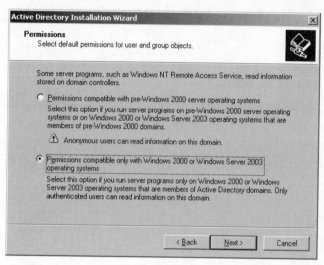

14. On the Directory Services Restore Mode Administrator Password page, type **P@ssw0rd**. Confirm the password in the Confirm Password box. Click Next.

15. The Summary page displays the options that you have selected by using the wizard, as shown in the following example. Review the contents of this page for accuracy, and then click Next. The wizard will take eight minutes or more to configure Active Directory components and install the DNS Server service.

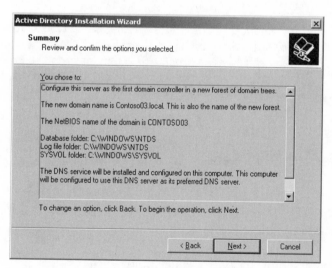

16. When the Completing The Active Directory Installation Wizard page appears, click Finish, and then click Restart Now.

> **NOTE** The Active Directory Installation Wizard should have completed two tasks that it occasionally fails to complete. First, the preferred DNS server needs to be set to 127.0.0.1. This can be checked by running Ipconfig /all at a command prompt. Second, SRV records need to be added to the DNS Server service. This can be forced by stopping and starting the netlogon service: at a command prompt, execute Net Stop Netlogon, followed by Net Start Netlogon.

EXERCISE 1-2: INSTALLING ACTIVE DIRECTORY USING AN ANSWER FILE

Estimated completion time: 20 minutes

You now want to create a replica domain controller in your test domain. In order to help eliminate human error when this task is completed on the actual domain, you intend to use an answer file, which you will test now. The following text is an example of what the answer file would look like for use on Computer02, with Computer01 being the initial domain controller in the forest.

```
[DCInstall]
RebootOnSuccess=Yes
DatabasePath=%systemroot%\ntds
LogPath=%systemroot%\ntds
SYSVOLPath=%systemroot%\sysvol
UserName=administrator
Password=P@ssw0rd
UserDomain=contoso01.local
ReplicaOrNewDomain=Replica
ReplicaDomainDNSName=contoso01.local
AdministratorPassword=P@ssw0rd
```

When you complete this task on the replica domain controllers in the actual domain (as opposed to the test domain), you intend to use a floppy disk for convenience. But for now you will access the answer file on the local hard drive.

NOTE For security reasons, when you use an answer file that contains passwords, the passwords will be removed when the answer file is used. This means that if something goes wrong and you must redo the promotion, you will either have to enter the passwords manually when prompted, or replace the passwords in the answer file.

IMPORTANT Complete this exercise on the even-numbered computer.

Setting the Preferred DNS Server to a DNS Server for the Domain

The following steps will set your preferred DNS Server address to the IP address of the odd-numbered computer in your domain.

1. From the Start menu, point to Control Panel, point to Network Connections, right-click Local Area Connection, and select Properties.

2. In the Local Area Connection Properties dialog box, select Internet Protocol (TCP/IP), and click Properties.

3. If there is a Preferred DNS Server entry that your computer relies on for Internet name resolution (your instructor will inform you if this is so), type that IP address into the Alternate DNS Server text box. In the Preferred DNS Server text box, type **10.1.1.zz**. An example is shown in the following figure. Click OK.

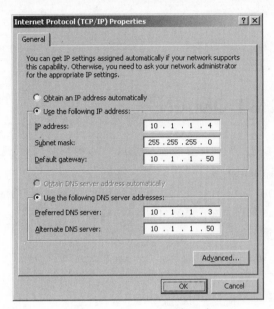

4. In the Local Area Connection Properties dialog box, click Close.

Installing Active Directory

The following steps will configure your computer as a replica domain controller for the Contoso*xx*.local domain, using an answer file.

1. From the Start menu, select Run.

2. In the Run dialog box, in the Open text box, type **dcpromo /answer: "c:\Lab Manual\Lab01\Computeryy\dc.txt"** and press ENTER.

> **CAUTION**   Be sure that you use quotes around your path as shown in step 2.

3. Provided that the information in your answer file is correct and the even-numbered computer can contact the DNS server on the odd-numbered computer, the Active Directory Installation Wizard will promote your computer to a replica domain controller. The new domain controller will restart after the promotion is complete.

NOTE   To create an answer file for use with Dcpromo, refer to the instructions located in "Microsoft Windows Preinstallation Reference" found in the Ref.chm file on the Windows Server 2003 CD. The Ref.chm file must be extracted from the Deploy.cab file in the \Support\Tools folder. Use the Index tab to search for DCInstall, the help topic that explains each of the entries that can be specified in the [DCInstall] section of the file.

QUESTION   What is the benefit of installing Active Directory using an answer file?

EXERCISE 1-3: RAISING THE DOMAIN FUNCTIONAL LEVEL

Estimated completion time: 5 minutes

To take full advantage of the improvements offered in Windows Server 2003, you will need to raise the domain and forest functional levels.

IMPORTANT   Complete this exercise on the odd-numbered computer.

1. Log on with your Administrator account.

2. From the Start menu, point to Administrative Tools, and select Active Directory Users And Computers.

3. In the Active Directory Users And Computers console, in the scope pane, right-click Contosoxx.local, and select Raise Domain Functional Level.

4. In the Raise Domain Functional Level dialog box, in the Select An Available Domain Functional Level drop-down list, as shown in the following figure, select Windows Server 2003, and then click Raise.

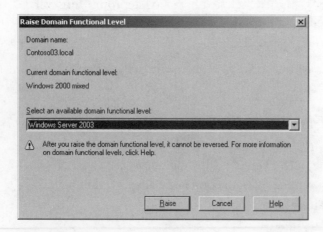

5. In the Raise Domain Functional Level message box, stating that the change is irreversible, click OK.

6. In the Raise Domain Functional Level message box, stating that the domain functional level was raised successfully, click OK

7. Close the Active Directory Users And Computers console.

EXERCISE 1-4: RAISING THE FOREST FUNCTIONAL LEVEL

Estimated completion time: 5 minutes

With the domain functional level raised, you can now raise the forest functional level to take full advantage of all new features offered.

IMPORTANT   *Complete this exercise on the even-numbered computer.*

1. Log on with your Administrator account.

2. From the Start menu, point to Administrative Tools, and then select Active Directory Domains And Trusts.

3. In the Active Directory Domains And Trusts console, in the scope pane, right-click the Active Directory Domains And Trusts node, and then click Raise Forest Functional Level.

4. In the Raise Forest Functional Level dialog box, as shown in the following figure, notice that the Select An Available Forest Functional Level drop-down list contains only one choice: Windows Server 2003. Click Raise.

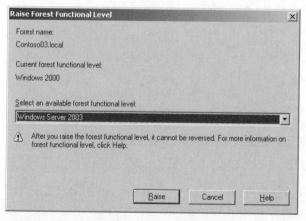

5. In the Raise Forest Functional Level message box, stating that the change is irreversible, click OK.

6. In the Raise Forest Functional Level message box, stating that the functional level was raised successfully, click OK.

7. Close the Active Directory Domains And Trusts console.

EXERCISE 1-5: CONFIGURING A GLOBAL CATALOG SERVER

Estimated completion time: 5 minutes

In order to achieve better reliability, you want to configure a second Global Catalog Server on the replica domain controller you configured earlier.

IMPORTANT   *Complete this exercise on the even-numbered computer.*

1. From the Start menu, point to Administrative Tools, and then select Active Directory Sites And Services.

2. In the Active Directory Sites And Services console, in the scope pane, expand Sites, Default-First-Site-Name, Servers, and then expand Computeryy, as shown below.

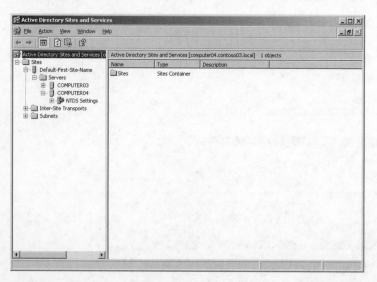

3. In the scope pane, right-click NTDS Settings, and select Properties.

4. In the NTDS Settings Properties dialog box, in the General tab, select the Global Catalog check box and click OK.

5. Close the Active Directory Sites And Services console.

EXERCISE 1-6: CONFIGURING UNIVERSAL GROUP CACHING

Estimated completion time: 5 minutes

In case you find it necessary on the actual domain to speed user authentication across domains, you want to configure universal group caching.

IMPORTANT   *Complete this exercise on the odd-numbered computer.*

1. From the Start menu, point to Administrative Tools, and then select Active Directory Sites And Services.

    In the Active Directory Sites And Services console, expand the Sites node.

2. Select Default-First-Site-Name to view its contents in the Details pane, as shown in the following example.

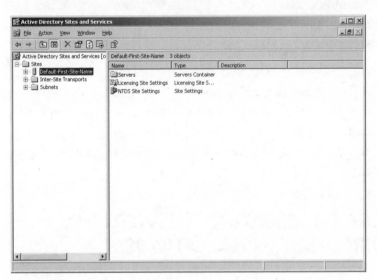

3. In the details pane, right-click NTDS Site Settings, and select Properties.

4. In the NTDS Site Settings Properties dialog box, in the Site Settings tab, select the Enable Universal Group Membership Caching check box.

    In the Refresh Cache From drop-down list, ensure that <Default> is selected. This will cause domain controllers in this site to refresh their cache from the nearest site that has a global catalog server. Click OK.

5. Close the Active Directory Sites And Services console.

LAB REVIEW QUESTIONS

Estimated completion time: 15 minutes

1. In Exercise 1-1, why were you asked to configure a domain in a new forest? Why didn't you configure a domain within an existing forest?

2. In which cases would you select alternate permissions for step 13 of Exercise 1-1?

3. Why won't the normal Administrator account password work in Directory Services Restore Mode?

4. Why does a domain controller hosting a DNS server require a static IP address?

5. If you had not set up the global catalog server in Exercise 1-5, how many global catalog servers would be present in your domain, and why?

6. What is a reason besides being able to look up information more quickly that you might want to configure a second global catalog server in a forest that has only one?

7. In order to speed user authentication, you set up a server local to your domain with universal group membership caching. A user's password is changed on the global catalog server that handles update requests from the local server you configured with universal group membership caching. An hour after the password has been changed, you are able to log on with the old password. Why?

LAB CHALLENGE 1-1: CREATING ANSWER FILES FOR ACTIVE DIRECTORY INSTALLATIONS

Estimated completion time: 25 minutes

Litware, Inc., is a subsidiary of Contoso, Ltd. Litware is a small company that has just recently become large enough to justify creating a domain. Windows Server 2003 has been installed on two computers. You are not at the Litware site (and therefore cannot run the Dcpromo wizard), and you need to create two answer files to automate the promotion of each of the systems to be domain controllers. The domain name should be Litware.local.

Write two answer files, one to create the first domain controller in a new forest, and a second answer file to promote a server to be a replica domain controller for the new domain.

LAB 2
ADVANCED MICROSOFT ACTIVE DIRECTORY CONCEPTS

This lab contains the following exercises and activities:

- Exercise 2-1: Using Ntdsutil

- Exercise 2-2: Creating a Trust Between Forests

- Exercise 2-3: Adding and Removing a User Principal Name Suffix

- Lab Review Questions

- Lab Challenge 2-1: Transferring the Schema Master Role

SCENARIO

After successfully completing the first phase of testing for the creation of a new Microsoft Windows Server 2003 Active Directory network, you have been directed by the chief information officer (CIO) of Contoso, Ltd., to begin exploring more advanced (and often lesser understood) Active Directory features. Contoso is interested in the possibility of using custom application directory partitions, and therefore you must be familiar with creating and removing application directory partitions, creating and removing application directory partition replicas, and examining application directory partition information.

Furthermore, two divisions of Contoso are merging, and you must configure trusts between the forests containing the domains. You also must work with UPN suffixes to create a new logon scheme. Finally, to perform maintenance on a domain controller hosting the Schema Master role, you must temporarily move the role to another domain controller.

After completing this lab, you will be able to:

- ■ Create or remove an application directory partition
- ■ Add or remove an application directory partition replica
- ■ Manage and examine application directory partition information
- ■ Add or remove user principal name (UPN) suffixes
- ■ Transfer the Schema Master role

Estimated completion time: 95 minutes

BEFORE YOU BEGIN

To complete this lab, you'll need to pair with the student that is a member of the same domain as you, as established in Lab 1.

This lab often refers to the number of your domain, your computer, or your partner's computer according to the following conventions:

- ■ *xx* is the number of your domain.
- ■ *yy* is the number of your computer.
- ■ *zz* is the number of your partner's computer.

For example, if you are using Computer04, *xx* = 03 (you are a member of Contoso03.local), *yy* = 04 (you are using Computer04), and *zz* = 03 (your partner is using Computer03).

In addition, in Exercise 2-2, you are required to form a group with another domain, so that the group contains four computers in two domains. The number of the other domain is referred to as *pp*. For example, if you are a member of Contoso01.local, and you pair with Contoso03.local, *pp* = 03.

EXERCISE 2-1: USING NTDSUTIL

Estimated completion time: 25 minutes

In this exercise, you perform various tasks concerning application directory partitions using the Ntdsutil command line utility.

Connecting to Your Server Using Ntdsutil

The following steps will connect to your server with the Ntdsutil utility.

1. Log on with your Administrator account (the password is **P@ssw0rd**).

2. From the Start menu, select Run.

3. In the Run dialog box, in the Open text box, type **cmd**, and then press ENTER.

4. In the command prompt window at the command prompt, type **ntdsutil**, and then press ENTER.

5. At the Ntdsutil prompt, type **domain management**, and then press ENTER.

6. At the Domain Management prompt, type **connection**, and then press ENTER.

7. At the Server Connections prompt, type **connect to server computeryy .contosoxx.local** and then press ENTER. An example of a successful connection is shown in the following example.

Creating Application Directory Partitions

The following steps use the Ntdsutil utility to create an application partition directory.

1. At the Server Connections prompt, type **quit**, and then press ENTER, to go back to the Domain Management prompt.

2. At the Domain Management prompt, type **create nc dc=appyy,dc= contosoxx,dc=local null**. An example of creating the application directory partition app03.contoso03.local is shown in the following figure.

QUESTION   What is the ramification of using the null value for the last parameter when creating a new application directory partition?

Deleting an Application Directory Partition

The following steps will delete the application directory partition that you created in the previous task.

1. Ensure that you are at the Domain Management prompt within the Ntdsutil utility.

2. At the Domain Management prompt, type **delete nc dc=appyy,dc= contosoxx,dc=local**. An example of a successfully deleted application directory partition is shown in the following figure.

Creating an Application Directory Partition Replica

In the following task, you will create application directory partition replicas. In order to do this, however, you are first asked to create new application directory partitions.

1. Create an application directory partition named newappyy (use the same technique as in the "Creating Application Directory Partition" section in this exercise).

   NOTE Wait until your partner has completed step 1 before continuing.

2. At the Domain Management prompt, type **add nc replica dc= newappzz,dc=contosoxx,dc=local null**. An example of creating the replica application directory partition newapp04.contoso03.local is shown in the following example.

Removing an Application Directory Partition Replica

The following steps remove the application directory partition replica that you created.

1. Ensure that you are at the Domain Management prompt within the Ntdsutil utility.

2. At the Domain Management prompt, type **remove nc replica dc=newappzz,dc=contosoxx,dc=local null**, which is the Distinguished Name (DN) of the replica application directory you created in the previous task. An example of a successfully removed replica application partition is shown in the following figure.

Viewing Application Directory Partition Information

The following steps will display various information about the application directory partitions within your installation of Active Directory.

1. At the Domain Management prompt, type **list**, and then press ENTER. An example listing in the following figure.

2. At the Domain Management prompt, type **list nc information dc= newapp*yy*,dc=contoso*xx*,dc=local**. An example of information revealed by the list and list nc commands is shown in the following figure.

3. Type **quit** and press ENTER, twice, to exit Ntdsutil.

4. Close the command prompt window.

EXERCISE 2-2: CREATING A TRUST BETWEEN FORESTS

Estimated completion time: 35 minutes

Two divisions within Contoso are going to merge in order to reduce overhead and thereby decrease their budgets. In order to accomplish this, management has decided not to merge the domains of the two divisions, but rather to create a trust between them.

IMPORTANT   In this exercise, each student pair comprising a domain must join together with another student pair to form a group with a pair of domains. The following exercise is completed only on the odd-numbered computer in each domain.

Configuring a DNS Forwarder

Before the trust can be established, in order to allow communication across the forests in which the trust will be created, you must configure DNS forwarders to handle cross-forest DNS name resolution.

1. From the Start menu, point to Administrative Tools and select DNS.

2. In the DNS console, in the scope pane, select and right-click Computeryy, and then select Properties.

3. In the Computeryy Properties dialog box, in the Forwarders tab, click New.

4. In the New Forwarder dialog box, in the DNS Domain text box, type **contoso*pp*.local.** Click OK.

5. In the Computeryy Properties dialog box, in the DNS Domain list box, ensure that Contoso*pp*.local is selected. In the Selected Domain's Forwarder IP Address List text box, type **10.1.1.*pp*.** Click Add.

6. Select the Do Not Use Recursion For This Domain check box. Click OK. Shown in the following figure is how the Computeryy Properties dialog box would look if you were configuring Computer01 to forward DNS requests to Computer03 for resolution of host names in the Contoso03.local domain.

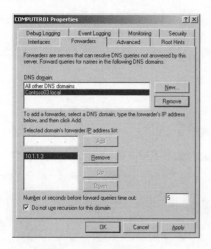

7. Close the DNS console.

Creating the First Side of the Trust

The trust that is being created between the newly merged divisions of Contoso should not be symmetrical for security reasons. The users of the lower-numbered domain have no reason to be able to access resources on the higher-numbered domain, and therefore only the higher-numbered domain is to be able to authenticate in the lower-numbered domain.

> **IMPORTANT**   The following steps should be completed on the even-numbered computer in the higher-numbered domain.

1. From the Start menu, point to Administrative Tools and select Active Directory Domains And Trusts.

2. In the Active Directory Domains And Trusts console, in the scope pane, right-click Contoso*xx*.local, and then select Properties.

3. In the Contoso*xx*.local Properties dialog box, in the Trusts tab (as shown in the following figure), click New Trust.

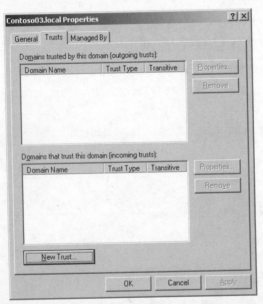

4. In the New Trusts Wizard, on the Welcome To The New Trust Wizard page, click Next.

5. On the Trust Name page, type **contoso*pp*.local**. Click Next.

6. On the Trust Type page, select Forest Trust, and then click Next.

7. On the Direction Of Trust page, select One-Way: Incoming, as shown in the following figure, and then click Next.

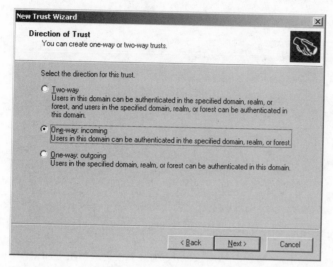

8. On the Sides Of Trust page, verify that This Domain Only is selected, and then click Next.

> **NOTE**   Ordinarily, you can save some work by selecting the Both This Domain And The Specified Domain option on the Sides Of Trust page. However, for instructional purposes, this lab pretends that you do not have access to an account on the other domain with the right to create trusts. The trust relationship is completed from the other domain later in this exercise.

9. On the Trust Password page, in the Trust Password and Confirm Trust Password text boxes, type **P@ssw0rd**. Click Next.

10. On the Trust Selections Complete page (an example is shown in the following figure), click Next.

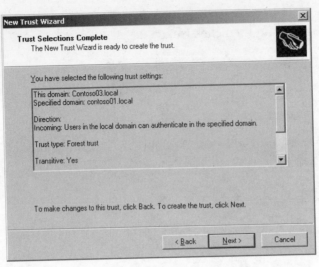

11. On the Trust Creation Complete page, click Next.

12. On the Confirm Incoming Trust page, verify that No, Do Not Confirm The Incoming Trust is selected, and then click Next.

13. On the Completing The New Trust Wizard page, click Finish.

14. In the Contosoxx.local Properties dialog box, click OK.

15. Close the Active Directory Domains And Trusts console.

Completing the Trust

The following steps will complete the trust begun in the previous task.

> **IMPORTANT** The following steps should be completed on the odd-numbered computer in the lower-numbered domain.

1. Open the Active Directory Domains And Trusts console.

2. In the Active Directory Domains And Trusts console, in the scope pane, select and right-click Contosoxx.local, and select Properties.

3. In the Contosoxx.local Properties dialog box, in the Trusts tab, click New Trust.

4. In the New Trust Wizard, on the Welcome To The New Trust Wizard page, click Next.

5. On the Trust Name page, in the Name text box, type **contoso*pp*.local** and click Next.

6. On the Trust Type page, select Forest Trust, and click Next.

7. On the Direction Of Trust page, select One-Way: Outgoing, and click Next.

8. On the Sides Of Trust page, ensure that This Domain Only is selected and click Next.

9. On the Outgoing Trust Authentication Level page, ensure that Forest-Wide Authentication is selected, and click Next.

10. On the Trust Password page, in the Trust Password and Confirm Trust Password text boxes, type **P@ssw0rd**. Click Next.

11. On the Trust Selections Complete page, click Next.

12. On the Trust Creation Complete page, click Next.

13. On the Confirm Outgoing Trust page, select Yes, Confirm The Outgoing Trust and click Next.

14. On the Completing The New Trust Wizard page (an example is shown in the following figure), click Finish.

15. In the Contoso*xx*.local Properties dialog box, click OK.

16. Close the Active Directory Domains And Trusts console.

Verifying the Trust

The following will verify that the trust has been completed by inspecting the options in the Log On To Windows dialog box.

1. Log off and press CTRL+ALT+DEL to open the Log On To Windows dialog box.

2. In the Log On To Windows dialog box, select the Log On To drop-down list.

QUESTION   What are the options listed in the Log On To drop-down list?

EXERCISE 2-3: ADDING AND REMOVING A USER PRINCIPAL NAME SUFFIX

Estimated completion time: 20 minutes

Contoso has recently acquired a small advertising firm to handle the bulk of its marketing needs internally. For organizational purposes, the employees of this new division need to log on to the same domain as everybody else, but with an alternate UPN suffix.

Adding a UPN Suffix

The following steps will create a new UPN suffix.

1. Log on with your Administrator account.

2. Open the Active Directory Domains And Trusts console.

3. In the Active Directory Domains And Trusts console, in the scope pane, select and right-click the Active Directory Domains And Trusts node, and select Properties.

4. In the Active Directory Domains And Trusts Properties dialog box, in the UPN Suffixes tab, in the Alternative UPN Suffixes text box, type **Marketingyy.Contosoxx.local** and then click Add. Click OK.

5. Close the Active Directory Domains And Trusts console.

Verifying the UPN Suffix

The following steps will create a new user account that will use the UPN suffix created in the previous task to log on.

1. From the Start menu, point to Adimistrative Tools and select Active Directory Users And Computers.

2. In the Active Directory Users And Computers console, expand Contoso*xx*.local and select Users.

3. From the Action menu, point to New and select User.

4. In the New Object - User dialog box, in the First Name text box, type **User**. In the Last Name text box, type **yy**. In the User Logon Name text box, type **Useryy**. In the drop-down list next to the User Logon Name text box, select Marketing*yy*.Contoso*xx*.local. An example is shown in the following figure. Click Next.

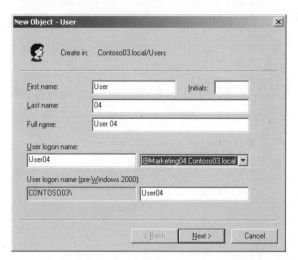

5. In the New Object - User dialog box, clear the User Must Change Password At Next Logon check box. In the Password and Confirm Password text boxes, type **P@ssw0rd**. Click Next. Click Finish.

6. In the Active Directory Users And Computers dialog box, verify that Users is selected in the scope pane. In the details pane, right-click User *yy* and select Properties.

7. In the User *yy* Properties dialog box, in the Member Of tab, click Add.

8. In the Select Groups dialog box, in the Enter The Object Names To Select (Examples) text box, type Admin and click Check Names. Administrators will appear underlined. Click OK.

9. In the User *yy* Properties dialog box, click OK.

10. Log off. Press CTRL+ALT+DEL to open the Log On To Windows dialog box.

11. In the Log On To Windows dialog box, in the User Name text box, type **Useryy@Marketingyy.Contosoxx.local**. In the Password text box, type **P@ssw0rd**. Click OK.

12. Log off and log back on with your Administrator account.

Removing a UPN Suffix

The following steps will remove the UPN suffix created earlier in this exercise.

1. Open the Active Directory Domains And Trusts Properties dialog box (steps 2 and 3 of the Adding a UPN Suffix section of this exercise).

2. In the Active Directories Domains And Trusts Properties dialog box, in the UPN Suffixes tab, select Marketingyy.Contosoxx.local, and click Remove.

3. In the Active Directory Domains And Trusts message box, click Yes to confirm that you want to delete the UPN suffix.

4. In the Active Directory Domains And Trusts Properties dialog box, click OK.

5. Close the Active Directory Domains And Trusts console.

LAB REVIEW QUESTIONS

Estimated completion time: 15 minutes

1. What is an application directory partition?

2. If your Active Directory forest contains a single domain named contoso .com and you create a new application directory partition using the distinguished name dc=appart1, where will this new partition be located?

3. What is the distinguished name of an application directory partition named ContosoDNSEast that is located in the root of the contoso.com domain?

4. Name and briefly explain the benefits of using an application directory partition.

5. What considerations should you make before deleting an application directory partition?

6. What commands are used to make and erase application directory partitions and application directory partition replicas?

LAB CHALLENGE 2-1: TRANSFERRING THE SCHEMA MASTER ROLE

Estimated completion time: 25 minutes

In making changes to the network at Contoso, the server currently hosting the Schema Master role is going to be temporarily removed for maintenance. In order to preserve the role, it needs to be temporarily transferred to another server.

Within your student pair, you need to move the Schema Master role from the odd-numbered computer to the even-numbered computer. This should be accomplished from the even-numbered computer. Once that task has been completed, you need to move it back from the even-numbered computer to the odd-numbered computer. This should be accomplished from the odd-numbered computer.

LAB 3
PLANNING A HOST NAME RESOLUTION STRATEGY

This lab contains the following exercises and activities:

- Exercise 3-1: Installing a DNS Server

- Exercise 3-2: Configuring Forwarding and Disabling Root Hints

- Exercise 3-3: Adding Multiple DNS Servers to the DNS Console

- Exercise 3-4: Forcing Active Directory Replication to the New DNS Server

- Exercise 3-5: Creating a Standard Primary Zone

- Exercise 3-6: Creating a Standard Secondary Zone

- Exercise 3-7: Specifying Name Servers to Allow Zone Transfers

- Exercise 3-8: Configuring Conditional Forwarding

- Exercise 3-9: Changing Zone Types and Securing Dynamic Updates

- Lab Review Questions

- Lab Challenge 3-1: Configuring Transfers Between Active Directory–
  Integrated Zones and Standard Zones

SCENARIO

Although Contoso, Ltd., is using a Microsoft Windows Server 2003 Active Directory forest for its production network, some of the software engineers are using UNIX computers for development and testing. You must therefore support UNIX Domain Name System (DNS) servers that host standard secondary copies of primary zones hosted on Windows Server 2003 DNS servers.

In addition, in order to increase security and stability, you need to configure conditional forwarding, disable root hints, and change DNS zone types so that you can configure secure DNS dynamic updates.

After completing this lab, you will be able to:

- Install the DNS service on a server
- Create Active Directory–integrated and standard DNS zones
- Configure zone transfers
- Configure conditional forwarding on DNS servers
- Configure options for DNS security
- Configure reverse lookup zones

Estimated completion time: 90 minutes

BEFORE YOU BEGIN

To complete this lab, you'll need to pair with the student that is a member of the same domain as you, as established in Lab 1.

This lab often refers to the number of your domain, your computer, or your partner's computer according to the following conventions:

- *xx* is the number of your domain.
- *yy* is the number of your computer.
- *zz* is the number of your partner's computer.

For example, if you are using Computer04, *xx* = 03 (you are a member of Contoso03.local), *yy* = 04 (you are using Computer04), and *zz* = 03 (your partner is using Computer03).

In addition, in Exercise 3-8, you are required to form a group with another domain, so that the group contains four computers in two domains. The number of the other domain is referred to as *pp*. For example, if you are a member of Contoso01.local, and you pair with Contoso03.local, *pp* = 03.

EXERCISE 3-1: INSTALLING A DNS SERVER

Estimated completion time: 10 minutes

Currently, Contoso is reliant on one DNS server for internal name resolution. In order to reduce the work load of the existing DNS server, as well as to provide redundancy, you need to create a new DNS server.

Installing a DNS Server

NOTE   *The odd-numbered computers already host a DNS server installed during the Active Directory installation in Lab 1, "Reviewing Microsoft Active Directory Concepts."*

Complete this task on the even-numbered computers. Ensure that your Windows Server 2003 CD is in your CD/DVD drive. If the Welcome To Microsoft Windows Server 2003 screen opens after you insert the CD, close it.

1. Log on with your Administrator account (the password is P@ssword).

2. From the Start menu, point to Control Panel, and then select Add Or Remove Programs.

3. In the Add Or Remove Programs dialog box, click the Add/Remove Windows Components icon on the left.

4. In the Windows Components Wizard, on the Windows Components page, in the Components list box, select Networking Services, but do not select the check box next to it (as shown in the following example), and then click Details.

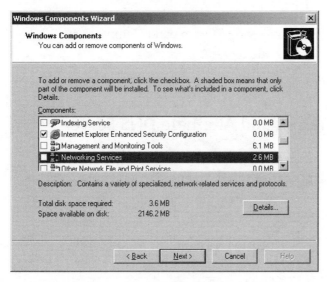

5. In the Networking Services dialog box, select the Domain Name System (DNS) check box. Click OK.

6. In the Windows Components Wizard, on the Windows Components page, the check box for Networking Services should be selected and shaded, as shown in the following example. Click Next.

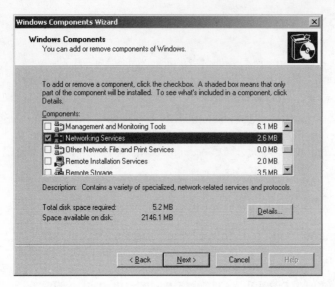

7. The Configuring Components page is displayed during installation. When the Completing The Windows Components Wizard page appears, click Finish.

8. Close the Add Or Remove Programs dialog box.

9. From the Start menu, point to Administrative Tools, and then select DNS.

10. In the DNS console, in the scope pane, expand Computeryy, and then select Forward Lookup Zones.

11. Leave the DNS console open for the next exercise.

Configuring Preferred and Alternate DNS Server IP Addresses

Now that your computer is a DNS server, you need to assign the local host as the preferred DNS server.

> **IMPORTANT** Complete the following task on both computers. The odd-numbered computers will already have the correct preferred DNS server configured.

1. From the Start menu, point to Control panel, point to Network Connections, right-click Local Area Connection, and then select Properties.

2. In the Local Area Connection Properties dialog box, select Internet Protocol (TCP/IP) and then click Properties.

3. In the Internet Protocol (TCP/IP) Properties dialog box, in the Preferred DNS Server text box, type **127.0.0.1**.

4. Clear the Alternate DNS Server text box (the next exercise will make it unnecessary). Click OK.

5. In the Local Area Connection Properties dialog box, click Close.

EXERCISE 3-2: CONFIGURING FORWARDING AND DISABLING ROOT HINTS

Estimated completion time: 5 minutes

Currently, Contoso relies on Internal DNS servers to provide external name resolution using iterative queries. In order to increase the security of your network, you want all external DNS name resolution to occur on a DNS server outside of the Contoso network. In order to do this, you need to forward all external DNS name resolution requests to an external DNS server, and you need to disable root hints on the internal DNS servers.

Configuring Forwarding

The following steps will configure your DNS server to forward external DNS requests to an external DNS server.

1. In the DNS console, in the scope pane, select and then right-click Computeryy, and then select Properties.

2. In the Computeryy Properties dialog box, in the Forwarders tab, in the DNS Domain list box, ensure that All Other DNS Domains is selected.

3. In the Selected Domain's Forwarder IP Address List text box, type the Internet Protocol (IP) address of a DNS server that can provide external DNS name resolution (your instructor will provide you with this IP address). Click Add. An example configuration is shown in the following figure. Click OK.

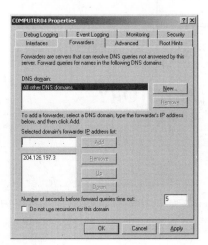

Disabling Root Hints

The following steps will disable your DNS server from using Root Hints to resolve external DNS name resolution requests by removing the root hints.

1. In the Root Hints tab, in the Name Servers list box, select the first line and click Remove.

2. Click Remove multiple times until the Name Servers list box is empty. Click OK.

EXERCISE 3-3: ADDING MULTIPLE DNS SERVERS TO THE DNS CONSOLE

Estimated completion time: 5 minutes

In this exercise, you add the other DNS server in your domain to the DNS Management console on your computer.

1. In the DNS console, in the scope pane, right-click DNS, and then select Connect To DNS Server.

2. In the Connect To DNS Server dialog box, select The Following Computer. In The Following Computer text box, type **Computer*zz* .contoso*xx*.local**. Ensure that the Connect To Specified Computer Now check box is selected, and then click OK. The following figure is an example of a DNS console attached to two DNS servers.

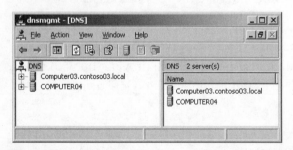

3. Leave the DNS console open for the next exercise.

EXERCISE 3-4: FORCING ACTIVE DIRECTORY REPLICATION TO THE NEW DNS SERVER

Estimated completion time: 10 minutes

You need to make sure that the Active Directory–integrated zones are replicated to the DNS server configured earlier in this lab. In order to do this, you will force replication and then check the forward lookup zones in the DNS console.

1. From the Start menu, point to Administrative Tools, and then select Active Directory Sites And Services.

2. In the Active Directory Sites And Services console, in the scope pane, expand Sites, expand Default-First-Site-Name, expand Servers, expand Computerzz, and select NTDS Settings.

3. In the details pane, right-click <Automatically Generated>, and then select Replicate Now.

4. In the Replicate Now message box confirming replication, click OK. Close the Active Directory Sites And Services console.

> **IMPORTANT**   Wait until your partner has completed step 4 before continuing. Complete the following step on the even-numbered computer only.

5. In the DNS console, in the scope pane, expand Computeryy, and then select Forward Lookup Zones.

> **QUESTION**   Which two forward lookup zones appear in the DNS console?

6. Leave the DNS console open for the following exercise.

EXERCISE 3-5: CREATING A STANDARD PRIMARY ZONE

Estimated completion time: 5 minutes

In this exercise, you create a standard primary zone on your partner's computer through the DNS console on your computer.

1. In the DNS console, in the scope pane, select and then right-click Computerzz.contosoxx.local, and then select New Zone.

2. In the New Zone Wizard, on the Welcome To The New Zone Wizard page, click Next.

3. On the Zone Type page, ensure that Primary Zone is selected, and clear the Store The Zone In Active Directory check box. Click Next.

4. On the Forward Or Reverse Zone page, ensure that Forward Lookup Zone is selected, and then click Next.

5. In the Zone Name box on the Zone Name page, type **Divisionyy .contosoxx.local**. An example is shown in the following figure. Click Next.

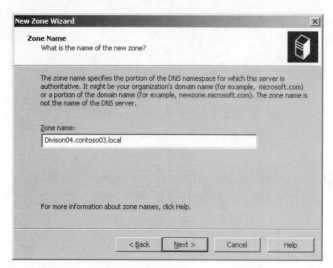

6. On the Zone File page, verify that Create A New File With This File Name is selected and that the file name is the zone name you entered in the previous step with .dns appended, as shown in the following figure. Click Next.

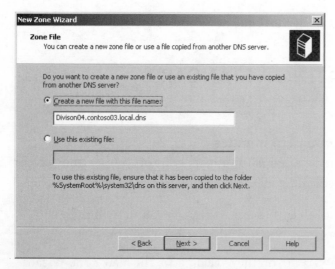

7. On the Dynamic Update page, select Allow Both Nonsecure And Secure Dynamic Updates (later in this lab you will configure the zone to allow only secure dynamic updates). Click Next.

8. On the Completing The New Zone Wizard page, read the summary. An example of this page is shown in the following figure. Click Finish.

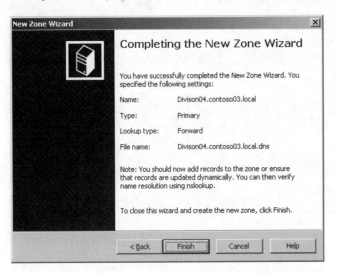

EXERCISE 3-6: CREATING A STANDARD SECONDARY ZONE

Estimated completion time: 15 minutes

Currently, the zone you created in the previous exercise is hosted only as a primary zone on a single server. In order to increase stability, and to divide the DNS server workload, you need to create a secondary zone on another DNS server.

> **NOTE** Do not continue until your partner has finished the previous exercise.

1. Close and open the DNS console to reload the zone files.

2. In the scope pane, select and then right-click Computeryy, and then select New Zone.

3. In the New Zone Wizard, on the Welcome To The New Zone Wizard page, click Next.

4. On the Zone Type page, select Secondary Zone, as shown in the following figure.

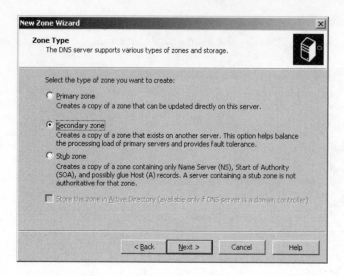

QUESTION   Why is the option to store the zone in Active Directory unavailable when you select Secondary Zone?

5. On the Zone Type page, click Next.

6. On the Forward Or Reverse Lookup Zone page, ensure Forward Lookup Zone is selected, and then click Next.

7. On the Zone Name page, click Browse.

8. In the Browse dialog box, in the Records list box, select Computer*zz* .contoso*xx*.local, and then click OK.

9. Select Forward Lookup Zones, and then click OK.

10. Select Division*yy*.contoso*xx*.local. An example from Computer04 is shown in the following figure. Click OK.

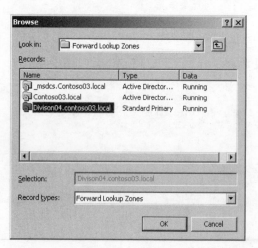

11. In the New Zone Wizard, on the Zone Name page, click Next.

12. On the Master DNS Servers page, click Browse.

13. In the Browse dialog box, select Computer*zz*.contoso*xx*.local. An example from Computer04 is shown in the following figure. Click OK.

14. In the New Zone Wizard, on the Master DNS Servers page, click Next.

15. On the Completing The New Zone Wizard page, review the summary. An example from Computer04 is shown in the following figure. Click Finish.

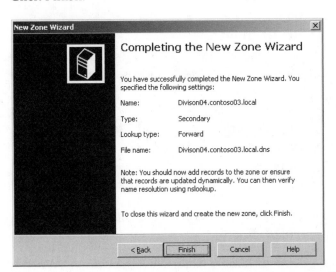

16. In the DNS console, in the scope pane, expand Computeryy, expand Forward Lookup Zones, and then select Divisionyy.contosoxx.local. An example from Computer04 is shown in the following figure.

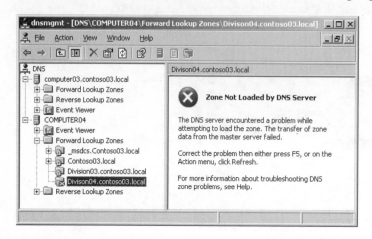

QUESTION   Why didn't the zone load?

17. Leave the DNS console open for the next exercise.

EXERCISE 3-7: SPECIFYING NAME SERVERS TO ALLOW ZONE TRANSFERS

Estimated completion time: 10 minutes

In order to allow the standard primary zone to transfer its contents to the standard secondary zone, the standard primary zone must be made aware of the DNS server hosting the secondary zone.

1. In the DNS console, in the scope pane, expand Computerzz .contosoxx.local, expand Forward Lookup Zones, select and then right-click Divisionyy.contosoxx.local, and then select Properties.

2. In the Divisonyy.contosoxx.local Properties dialog box, select the Name Servers tab, and then click Add.

3. In the Server Fully Qualified Domain Name (FQDN) text box, type **Computeryy.contosoxx.local**. In the IP Address text box, type **10.1.1.yy**, and then click Add. An example from Computer04 is shown in the following figure. Click OK.

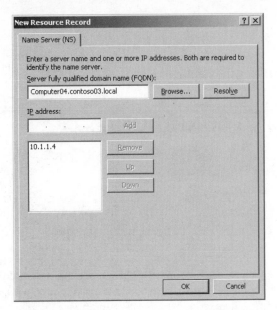

4. In the Divisonyy.contosoxx.local Properties dialog box, click OK.

5. In the DNS console, in the scope pane, expand Computeryy, expand
   Forward Lookup Zones, select and then right-click the Divisionyy
   .contosoxx.local and select Transfer From Master.

> **NOTE** You might have to repeat this step several times over the course
> of a minute before the zone transfers. An example after the zone has
> loaded is shown in the following figure.

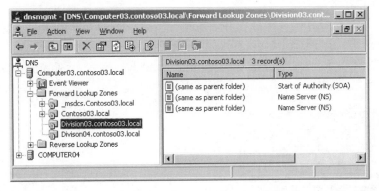

6. Take a moment to browse the properties of the forward lookup zones
   hosted on your server.

> **QUESTION** Which functions on the Action menu are available for
> secondary zones that are not available on the Action menu for the
> primary zone?

QUESTION   *Can you create or configure resource records for the secondary zone?*

7. Leave the DNS console open for the next exercise.

EXERCISE 3-8: CONFIGURING CONDITIONAL FORWARDING

Estimated completion time: 5 minutes

In order to allow cross-forest DNS name resolution between two forests within the Contoso network, you need to configure a conditional forwarder.

IMPORTANT   *In this exercise, each student pair comprising a domain must join together with another student pair to form a group with a pair of domains. Complete the following exercise on the even-numbered computers, or on all the computers if Exercise 2-2, "Creating a Trust Between Forests", has not been completed in Lab 2, "Advanced Microsoft Active Directory Concepts."*

1. In the DNS console, in the scope pane, right-click Computer*yy*, and then select Properties.

2. In the Computer*yy* Properties dialog box, in the Forwarders tab, click New.

3. In the New Forwarder dialog box, in the DNS Domain text box, type **Contoso*pp*.local**. Click OK.

4. In the Computer*yy* Properties dialog box, in the Selected Domain's Forwarder IP Address List text box, type **10.1.1.*pp***. Click Add. Select the Do Not Use Recursion For This Domain check box. An example is pictured in the following figure. Click OK.

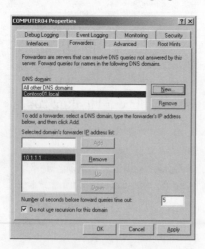

5. Leave the DNS console open for the next exercise.

EXERCISE 3-9: CHANGING ZONE TYPES AND SECURING DYNAMIC UPDATES

Estimated completion time: 10 minutes

You have been asked to bolster security concerning DNS servers on the network. In order to do this, you need to secure DNS dynamic updates.

Changing Zone Types to Active Directory–Integrated

1. In order to secure DNS dynamic updates, you need to first change zone types to Active Directory–integrated.

2. In the DNS console, in the scope pane, expand Computeryy, expand Forward Lookup Zones, and then select and right-click Divisionzz .contosoxx.local, and select Properties, as shown in the following figure from Computer04.

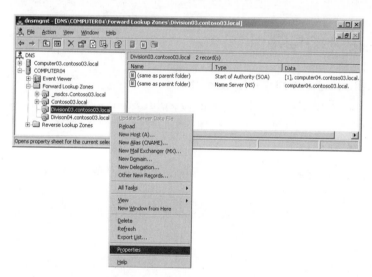

3. In the Divisionzz.contosoxx.local Properties dialog box, in the General tab, click Change.

> **QUESTION**   What options are currently available for dynamic updates?

4. In the Change Zone Type dialog box, select the Store The Zone In Active Directory (Available Only If DNS Server Is A Domain Controller) check box. Click OK.

5. In the DNS message box asking if you want the zone to become Active Directory–integrated, click Yes. Leave everything as is for the next task.

Securing Dynamic Updates

1. In the Division*zz*.contos*xx*.local Properties dialog box, in the Dynamic Updates drop-down list, select Secure Only. Click OK.

2. Close the DNS console.

> **QUESTION**   What are some of the benefits of using Active Directory–integrated zones?

> **QUESTION**   Before you have the option of configuring Secure Only dynamic updates on a Windows Server 2003 DNS server, what must be true of the associated DNS zone?

LAB REVIEW QUESTIONS

Estimated completion time: 15 minutes

1. How can forwarding external DNS name resolution requests (originating from an internal network) to an outside DNS server increase security?

2. You have configured a standard secondary zone on a DNS server running Windows Server 2003 for a remote office location. The secondary zone on this DNS server is not receiving zone transfers from the Active Directory–integrated zone configured as its primary. What is the likely cause of this problem?

3. Your colleague configured a standard primary DNS zone. Later, you want to enable Secure Only dynamic updates, but the option isn't available. What must you do in order for this option to be available?

4. If a DNS server were also a domain controller, would you be able to create a secondary zone with the same name as an existing Active Directory–integrated zone?

5. How many standard secondary zones can be created from a single standard primary zone?

LAB CHALLENGE 3-1: CONFIGURING TRANSFERS BETWEEN ACTIVE DIRECTORY–INTEGRATED ZONES AND STANDARD ZONES

Estimated completion time: 20 minutes

> **IMPORTANT**   The Lab Challenge solution requires the participation of both computers in your domain. Students should work in pairs to solve the challenge.

A DNS problem has been found on the network at Contoso. When resource records are added to Active Directory–integrated zones, the standard secondary zones are not reflecting the new records, even after ample time has passed (before you changed the Active Directory–integrated zones from standard primary zones, replication was working fine). You must verify this behavior by adding a faux resource record to one of the Active Directory–integrated zones that you created earlier in the lab and by trying to force the corresponding standard secondary zone to load the new data. Once you have verified the problem, you must solve it while maximizing security. Verify that you have successfully solved the problem by observing the faux resource record that you create in the Active Directory–integrated zone propagate to the standard secondary zone.

GROUP POLICY STRATEGY

This lab contains the following exercises and activities:

- Exercise 4-1: Creating and Editing Group Policy Objects

- Exercise 4-2: Linking Group Policy Objects

- Exercise 4-3: Filtering Group Policy Scope Using Security Groups

- Exercise 4-4: Testing Group Policy Settings Using a Test Account

- Exercise 4-5: Configuring Group Policy Application Exceptions

- Exercise 4-6: Configuring and Testing Folder Redirection

- Lab Review Questions

- Lab Challenge 4-1: Using the Group Policy Management Console

SCENARIO

After successfully installing and configuring the Active Directory directory service and Domain Name System (DNS) on your test systems, you decide that it is time to consider Group Policy. You want to use Group Policy to configure many settings for both users and computers throughout the forest. To accomplish this, you have decided to first create and test both organizational units (OUs) and GPOs. This testing will include creating new OUs and GPOs, linking GPOs, filtering GPO application according to security group, and applying exceptions to GPO application according to inheritance. You will also investigate redirection of the My Documents folder so that users can access My Documents from any computer in the network on a network share. You will test these settings by creating a test account.

After completing this lab, you will be able to:

- Create a new Group Policy Object (GPO)
- Edit a new or existing GPO
- Link and unlink GPOs
- Filter GPO application by using security groups
- Control GPO processing by using exceptions
- Configure and manage folder redirection
- Use the GPMC to audit Group Policy

Estimated completion time: 100 minutes

BEFORE YOU BEGIN

To complete this lab, you'll need to pair with the student that is a member of the same domain as you, as established in Lab 1.

This lab often refers to the number of your domain, your computer, or your partner's computer according to the following conventions:

- *xx* is the number of your domain.
- *yy* is the number of your computer.
- *zz* is the number of your partner's computer.

For example, if you are using Computer04, *xx* = 03 (you are a member of Contoso03.local), *yy* = 04 (you are using Computer04), and *zz* = 03 (your partner is using Computer03).

EXERCISE 4-1: CREATING AND EDITING GROUP POLICY OBJECTS

Estimated completion time: 10 minutes

Before implementing security on the network, you must first create OUs and GPOs. In the following exercise, you create both.

1. Log on with your Administrator account (the password is P@ssw0rd).

2. From the Start menu, point to Administrative Tools, and then select Active Directory Users And Computers.

3. In the Active Directory Users And Computers console, in the scope pane, select and then right-click Contoso*xx*.local, point to New, and then select Organizational Unit.

4. In the New Object - Organizational Unit dialog box, in the Name text box, type **OUyy**. An example from the perspective of Computer04 is shown below. Click OK.

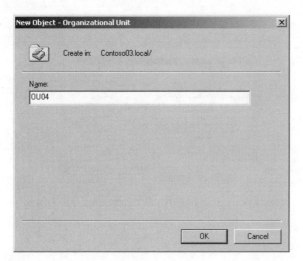

5. In the Active Directory Users And Computers console, in the scope pane, under Contoso*xx*.local, right-click OUyy and then select Properties.

> **NOTE** Step 6 might fail on the even-numbered computers if the OU has not yet replicated to the odd-numbered domain controller in your domain. You can either wait for replication to occur normally (about 20 seconds), or you can force replication in the Active Directory Sites And Services console, as explained in Exercise 3-4, "Forcing Active Directory Replication to the New DNS Server."

6. In the OUyy Properties dialog box, in the Group Policy tab, click New. For the name of the GPO, type **Workstation Policy yy**. Click Edit.

> **IMPORTANT** Complete steps 7 through 9 on the odd-numbered computer only.

7. In the Group Policy Object Editor, in the scope pane, under the User Configuration node, expand Administrative Templates, and then select the Start Menu And Taskbar node, as seen in the following figure. In the Details pane, double-click Remove Search Menu From Start Menu.

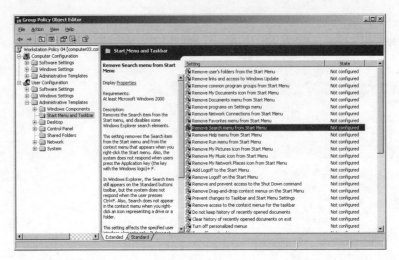

8. In the Remove Search Menu From Start Menu Properties dialog box, select the Explain tab and read the explanation.

> **QUESTION**   How are the following affected by enabling this setting: the Start menu context menu, Windows Explorer, and Internet Explorer?

> **IMPORTANT**   Complete steps 9 through 11 on the even-numbered computer only.

9. In the Setting tab, select Enabled, and then click OK.

10. In the Group Policy Object Editor, in the scope pane, under the User Configuration node, expand Administrative Templates, expand System, and then select Ctrl+Alt+Del Options. In the details pane, double-click Remove Lock Computer.

11. In the Remove Lock Computer Properties dialog box, select the Explain tab and read the explanation.

> **QUESTION**   What will happen when you enable this setting?

12. In the Settings tab, select Enabled, and then click OK.

> **IMPORTANT**   Complete steps 13 through 15 on both computers.

13. Close the Group Policy Object Editor.

14. Close the OUyy Properties dialog box.

15. Leave the Active Directory Users And Computers console open for the next exercise.

> **QUESTION**   *Do the settings you just applied affect users or computers, and why?*

EXERCISE 4-2: LINKING GROUP POLICY OBJECTS

Estimated completion time: 5 minutes

After creating two GPOs between you and your partner, you decide that it would be beneficial if both GPOs applied to both the OUs that have been created. The following steps link the GPO you created to the OU your partner created.

1. In the Active Directory Users And Computers console, in the scope pane, expand Contosoxx.local, right-click OUyy, and select Properties.

2. In the OUyy Properties dialog box, in the Group Policy tab, click Add.

3. In the Add Group Policy Object Link dialog box, in the All tab, in the All Group Policy Objects Stored In This Domain list box, select Workstation Policy *zz*, as shown in the following figure from Computer04. Click OK.

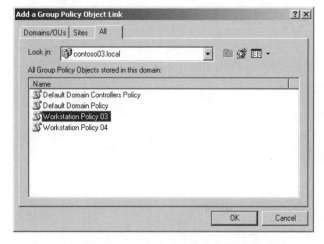

4. In the OUyy Properties dialog box, click OK.

5. Leave the Active Directory Users And Computers console open for the next exercise.

> **QUESTION**   *What is a benefit of linking an existing GPO to a container versus creating a new GPO with the same settings?*

EXERCISE 4-3: FILTERING GROUP POLICY SCOPE USING SECURITY GROUPS

Estimated completion time: 10 minutes

Although you are satisfied with the new GPOs you have created, you do not want all users to be restricted by the settings. Specifically, you want members of the Enterprise Admins group to be free of the restrictions. Also, in order to reduce computer start times, you need to disable the GPO from applying computer configuration settings.

1. In the Active Directory Users And Computers console, in the scope pane, expand Contoso*xx*.local, select and then right-click OU*yy*, and then select Properties.

2. In the OU*yy* Properties dialog box, in the Group Policy tab, select Workstation Policy *yy*, and then click Properties.

3. In the Workstation Policy *yy* Properties dialog box, in the General tab, select the Disable Computer Configuration Settings check box.

4. In the Confirm Disable message box, click Yes to confirm.

5. In the Workstation Policy *yy* Properties dialog box, in the Security tab, in the Group Or User Names list box, select Enterprise Admins (CONTOSO*xx*\Enterprise Admins).

6. In the Permissions For Enterprise Admins list box, select the Deny check box for the Apply Group Policy permission, as shown in the following figure. Click OK.

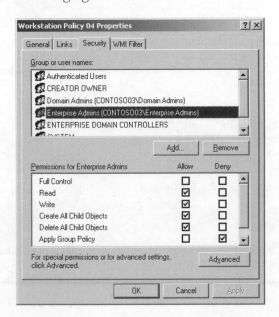

QUESTION   What happens when a permission is both allowed and denied to a user through different group memberships?

7. In the Security message box, click Yes to indicate you want to continue.

8. In the OUyy Properties dialog box, click OK.

9. Leave the Active Directory Users And Computers console open for the next exercise.

EXERCISE 4-4: TESTING GROUP POLICY SETTINGS USING A TEST ACCOUNT

Estimated completion time: 25 minutes

Now that you have completed forming the first OUs and GPOs for the domain, you want to observe the effects on a user account.

The following exercise creates a test account to observe the effects of applying a GPO to an OU to which the test account belongs.

1. In the Active Directory Users And Computers console, expand Contoso*xx*.local, and then select OUyy.

2. On the Action menu, point to New, and then select User.

3. In the New Object – User dialog box, in the First Name text box, type **Test**.

4. In the User Logon Name text box, type **Testyy**, and then click Next.

5. In the New Object – User dialog box, in the Password and Confirm Password text boxes, type **P@ssw0rd** (the 0 character is a zero). Clear the User Must Change Password At Next Logon check box. Click Next, and then click Finish.

6. In the Active Directory Users And Computers console, in the details pane, right-click Test, and select Add To A Group.

7. In the Select Group dialog box, in the Enter The Object Name To Select (Examples) text box, type **En** and Click Check Names. Enterprise Admins will appear underlined. Click OK.

8. In the Active Directory message box confirming that the operation was successful, click OK.

NOTE Steps 9 through 16 will allow members of the Domain Users group to log on to your computer. This is necessary because the Test account that you have created will be a member only of the Domain Users group later in this exercise, and will need to log on locally.

9. From the Start menu, point to Administrative Tools, and select Domain Controller Security Policy.

10. In the Default Domain Controller Security Settings console, expand Local Policies, and select User Rights Assignment.

11. In the Details pane, double-click Allow Log On Locally.

12. In the Allow Log On Locally Properties dialog box, click Add User Or Group.

13. In the Add User Or Group dialog box, click Browse.

14. In the Select Users, Computers, or Groups dialog box, in the Enter The Object To Select (Examples) text box, type **Domain U** and click Check Names. Domain Users will appear underlined. Click OK.

15. In the Add User Or Group dialog box, click OK.

16. In the Allow Log On Locally Properties dialog box, click OK.

17. Log on with the Test account you just created.

18. Click Start. Note that the Search shortcut is displayed in the Start menu.

19. Press CTRL+ALT+DEL. Note that the Lock Computer button is active. Click Cancel.

20. In the Active Directory Users And Computers console, in the scope pane, ensure that OUyy is selected under the Contosoxx.lcoal node. In the details pane, right-click Test, and select Properties.

21. In the Test Properties dialog box, in the Member Of tab, in the Member Of list box, select Enterprise Admins and click Remove.

22. In the Remove User From Group dialog box, click Yes to confirm the removal.

23. In the Test Properties dialog box, click OK.

24. Log on with your Test account.

TIP When you log on, the user's settings will refresh according to group policy and the user's access token will be updated.

25. Click Start. Note that the Search shortcut is not present.

26. Press CTRL+ALT+DEL. The Lock Computer button is unavailable.

QUESTION   *Specifically, why are these options no longer available?*

EXERCISE 4-5: CONFIGURING GROUP POLICY APPLICATION EXCEPTIONS

Estimated completion time: 10 minutes

You realize that policies set in a parent domain could negatively affect the policies you are trying to implement. You want to ensure that this does not occur, and you also want to ensure that the policies you have created are not overridden by policies defined elsewhere.

In this exercise, you confirm that the GPO you created is set to block policy inheritance, and you set the GPO to disallow overrides.

1. Log on with your Administrator account.

2. In the Active Directory Users And Computers console, in the scope pane, expand Contosoxx.local, select and then right-click OUyy, and then select Properties.

3. In the OUyy Properties dialog box, in the Group Policy tab, ensure that Workstation Policy yy is selected. Select the Block Policy Inheritance check box, as shown from Computer04 in the following figure.

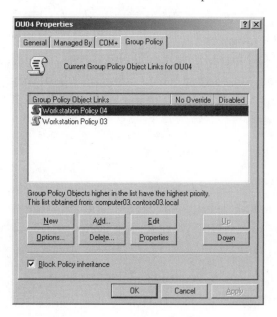

QUESTION   What is the effect of selecting Block Policy Inheritance?

QUESTION   Can applying the Block Policy Inheritance exception affect the application of policies linked to sites, domains, or organizational units above the site, domain, or organizational unit to which the block is applied?

4. Click Options.

5. In the Workstation Policy *yy* Options dialog box, select the No Override: Prevents Other Group Policy Objects From Overriding Policy Set In This One check box, as shown in the following figure. Click OK.

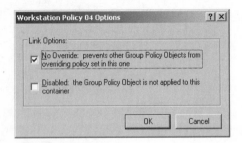

6. In the OU*yy* Properties dialog box, click OK.

7. Leave the Active Directory Users And Computers console open for the next exercise.

EXERCISE 4-6: CONFIGURING AND TESTING FOLDER REDIRECTION

Estimated completion time: 25 minutes

Some of the employees at Contoso often log on at different computers and want to have access to their documents. Rather than having users save all of their documents to a generic network share, you decide to implement folder redirection for their My Documents folders.

1. From the Start menu, select My Computer.

2. In My Computer, open Local Disk (C:).

3. In the C:\ window, from the File menu, point to New, and then select Folder. For the name of the folder, type **Workstation Policy *zz* Documents**, and press ENTER.

4. Right-click the Workstation Policy *zz* Documents folder you just created, and select Properties.

5. In the Workstation Policy *zz* Documents Properties dialog box, in the Sharing tab, select Share This Folder, as shown in the following figure. Click OK.

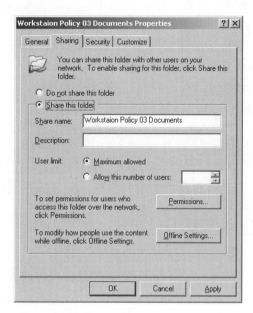

6. Close the C:\ window.

> **IMPORTANT** Wait until your partner has completed step 6 before continuing.

7. In the Active Directory Users And Computers console, in the scope pane, expand Contos*xx*.local, select and then right-click OU*yy*, and then select Properties.

8. In the OU*yy* Properties dialog box, in the Group Policy tab, ensure that Workstation Policy *yy* is selected. Click Edit.

9. In the Group Policy Object Editor, in the scope pane, expand User Configuration, expand Windows Settings, and select Folder Redirection.

10. In the Details pane, right-click My Documents, and then select Properties.

11. In the My Documents Properties dialog box, in the Setting drop-down list, select Basic – Redirect Everyone's Folder To The Same Location.

12. In the Target Folder Location drop-down list, ensure that Create A Folder For Each User Under The Root Path is selected.

13. In the Root Path text box, type **\\Computer*zz*\Workstation Policy *yy* Documents**, as seen in the following figure from Computer04. Click OK.

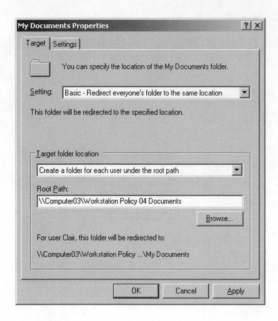

> **TIP**   Alternatively, you can browse to the location, which will eliminate potential typing errors.

14. Close the Group Policy Object Editor.

15. In the OUyy Properties dialog box, click OK.

Testing and Repairing the Folder Redirection

The following steps will test to see if the folder redirection is working.

1. Log on using your Test account.

2. From the Start menu, select Run.

3. In the Run dialog box, in the Open text box, type **\\Computerzz \Workstation Policy yy Documents**. Click OK.

4. From the View menu, click Refresh.

> **QUESTION**   How do we know that the folder redirection has failed?

5. On the Start menu, point to Administrative Tools, and select Event Viewer.

6. In the Event Viewer console, in the scope pane, select Application. Note in the details pane the error concerning folder redirection, as shown in the following figure. Double-click the folder redirection error event.

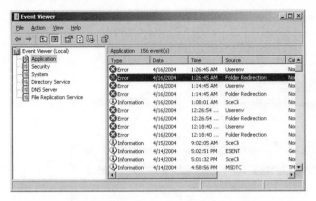

7. In the Event Properties, read the description of the event. An example is shown in the following figure. Click OK.

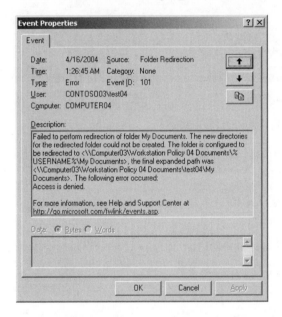

QUESTION What is preventing the folder redirection from working?

8. Log on with your Administrator account.

9. Open the C:\ folder, right-click the Workstation Policy *zz* Documents folder, and then select Properties.

10. In the Workstation Policy *zz* Documents Properties dialog box, in the Sharing tab, click Permissions.

11. In the Permissions For Workstation Policy *zz* Documents dialog box, click Add.

12. In the Select Users, Computers, Or Groups dialog box, in the Enter The Object To Select (Examples) text box, type **test**, and then click Check Names.

13. In the Multiple Names Found dialog box, in the Matching Names dialog box, select the Test account with the user name Testzz, as shown from Computer04 in the following figure. Click OK.

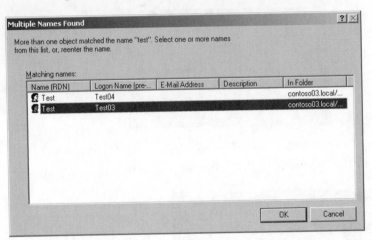

14. In the Select Users, Computers, Or Groups dialog box, click OK.

15. In the Permissions For Workstation Policy *zz* Documents dialog box, ensure that in Groups Or User Names list box, Test is selected.

16. In the Permissions For Test list box, select the Allow check box for the Full Control permission. Click OK.

17. In the Workstation Policy *zz* Documents Properties dialog box, click OK.

> **QUESTION** If you want to assign the Full Control permission to many accounts, what would be a better way of doing it than assigning the permission individually?

> **IMPORTANT** Wait until your partner has completed step 17, and then continue.

18. Log on with your Test account.

19. In the Run dialog box, in the Open text box, type **Computerzz** **Worksation Policy yy Documents**. Click OK. A folder containing a folder named \Testyy should appear.

LAB REVIEW QUESTIONS

Estimated completion time: 15 minutes

1. What is a GPO?

2. What are the two primary groupings of policy settings, and how are they used?

3. What is the difference between Block Policy Inheritance and No Override?

4. How do you prevent a GPO from applying to a specific group?

5. You want to block application of all Group Policy settings that reach the North OU from all of the OU's parent objects. To accomplish this, which exception do you apply and where?

6. You want to ensure that none of the South OU desktop settings applied to the South OU can be overridden. To accomplish this, which exception do you apply and where?

LAB CHALLENGE 4-1: USING THE GROUP POLICY MANAGEMENT CONSOLE

Estimated completion time: 35 minutes

You are a new domain administrator at Contoso and have been put in charge of reforming Group Policy across the domain. After interviewing other technicians, you realize that nobody is really aware of all the Group Policy settings, and from where they come. Therefore, to audit the Group Policy settings, you will use the Group Policy Management Console (GPMC).

You must install the Group Policy Management Console (GPMC) using the Gpmc.msi installer package. To install GPMC, run Gpmc.msi, which is located in the C:\Lab Manual\Lab04 folder, and follow the on-screen instructions.

Once you have installed GPMC, use it to determine the group policy results for both your Test and Administrator accounts. Also use it to model the group policy of OUyy and OUzz.

> **IMPORTANT** In order to model the group policy of the OUs, you must disable the block policy inheritance exception. Otherwise, the wizard cannot access the OUs. Once you have completed the challenge, re-configure the exception.

Once you have completed these audits, use the results to answer the following questions.

> **QUESTION** Why are the group policy modeling results essentially the same for both OUs?

> **QUESTION** There is a subtle difference between the links of the GPOs to OUyy and OUzz that will determine how conflicting policies are applied. What is that difference?

QUESTION   The GPOs that are linked to the OUs you created define two policies. Where in the OUyy On OUyy modeling results are these policies reported?

QUESTION   According to the information in the Settings tab of the group policy results for your Test account, what is the winning GPO that assigns members of the Authenticated Users group the Add Workstation To Domain policy?

QUESTION   What user configuration settings have been applied to your Administrator account?

SOFTWARE DEPLOYMENT AND RESTRICTIONS USING GROUP POLICY

This lab contains the following exercises and activities:

- Exercise 5-1: Creating an SDP in a Trusted Forest
- Exercise 5-2: Publishing Software to Users Through Group Policy
- Exercise 5-3: Assigning Software to Users Through Group Policy
- Exercise 5-4: Removing Software Through Group Policy
- Exercise 5-5: Restricting Software Through Group Policy Using Paths
- Exercise 5-6: Restricting Software Through Group Policy Using a Hash
- Lab Review Questions
- Lab Challenge 5-1: Assigning Software to Computers
- Lab Challenge 5-2: Understanding How Hash Restrictions Work

SCENARIO

Currently, when software is distributed at Contoso, a technician has to visit each computer on which the software is being installed.

To increase efficiency, you want to configure Group Policy to deploy software for you. Furthermore, you want to use Group Policy to restrict user access to software that is either dangerous or distracting.

After completing this lab, you will be able to:

- Create a software distribution point (SDP) in another forest
- Publish and assign software to users through Group Policy
- Assign software to computers through Group Policy
- Restrict software using paths and hashes through Group Policy

Estimated completion time: 85 minutes

BEFORE YOU BEGIN

To complete this lab, you must ensure that the following dependencies are completed:

- A trust must be configured according to the specifications in Lab 2, "Advanced Microsoft Active Directory Concepts," Exercise 2-2, "Creating a Trust Between Forests." This will also configure cross-forest Domain Name System (DNS) name resolution.

- The Domain Users group is assigned the Log On Locally right. Exercise 4-4, "Testing Group Policy Settings Using a Test Account," steps 9 through 15 explain how to do this.

- You must install the Group Policy Management Console (GPMC) using the Gpmc.msi installer package, if you did not do so in the Lab Challenge 4-1 for Lab 4. To install GPMC, simply run Gpmc.msi, which is located in the C:\Lab Manual\Lab04 folder, and follow the on-screen instructions.

In this lab, you'll need to pair with the student that is a member of the same domain as you, as established in Lab 1, "Reviewing Microsoft Active Directory Concepts."

This lab often refers to the number of your domain, your computer, or your partner's computer according to the following conventions:

- *xx* is the number of your domain.
- *yy* is the number of your computer.
- *zz* is the number of your partner's computer.

For example, if you are using Computer04, *xx* = 03 (you are a member of Contoso03.local), *yy* = 04 (you are using Computer04), and *zz* = 03 (your partner is using Computer03).

In addition, you are required to form a group with another domain, so that the group contains four computers in two domains. The number of the other domain is referred to as *pp*. For example, if you are a member of Contoso01.local, and you pair with Contoso03.local, *pp* = 03.

Finally, you need to run the ADUCUpdate*xx*.vbs file located in C:\Lab Manual\Lab05 on either computer in your domain, but not both. This script will create a structure like that in Figure 5-1.

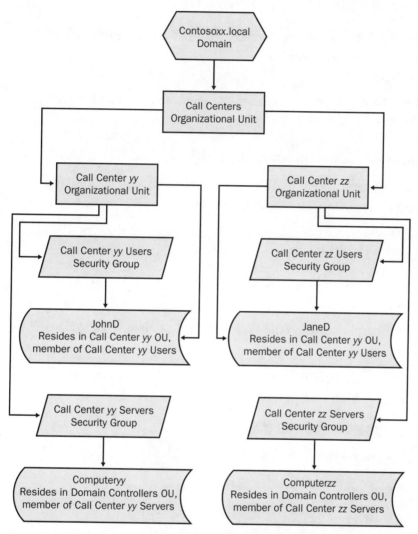

Figure 5-1   The ADUCUpdate*xx*.vbs script creates this structure within Active Directory

IMPORTANT   The ADUCUpdate*xx*.vbs script must be run, or the structure pictured in Figure 5-1 must be created manually, to complete this lab. This dependency is independent of Labs 1 through 4.

EXERCISE 5-1: CREATING AN SDP IN A TRUSTED FOREST

Estimated completion time: 20 minutes

Because you have recently upgraded all your servers to run Microsoft Windows Server 2003, you can create an SDP in a different forest as long as there is a two-way trust between the forest where it is located and the forest that is using it.

Rather than duplicate an SDP in two forests, you are going to create an SDP in one forest that is accessible to the two forests that will require it.

Converting the Trust to a Two-Way Trust

The following steps will convert the one-way trust between Contoso*xx*.local and Contoso*pp*.local to a two-way trust.

> **IMPORTANT**   *Complete the following steps on the even-numbered computer in the higher-numbered domain only.*

1. Log on with your Administrator account (the password is P@ssw0rd).

2. From the Start menu, point to All Programs, Administrative Tools, and then select Active Directory Domains And Trusts.

3. In the Active Directory Domains And Trusts console, in the scope pane, select and right-click Contoso*xx*.local, and then select Properties.

4. In the Contoso*xx*.local Properties dialog box, in the Trusts tab, click New Trust.

5. In the New Trust Wizard, on the Welcome To The New Trust Wizard page, click Next.

6. On the Trust Name page, type **Contoso*pp*.local**, as shown in the following example from Computer04, and then click Next.

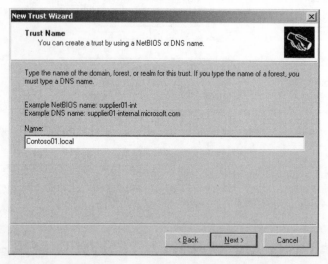

7. On the Existing One-Way Trust page, select Yes, Convert This Trust Into A Two-Way Trust. Click Next.

8. On the Sides Of Trust page, select the Both This Domain And The Specified Domain, and click Next.

9. In the User Name And Password page, enter your Administrator credentials, and click Next.

10. On the Outgoing Trust Authentication Level–Local Forest page, verify Forest-Wide Authentication is selected, and then click Next.

11. On the Trust Selections Complete page, click Next.

12. On the Trust Creation Complete page, click Next.

13. On the Confirm Outgoing Trust page, select Yes, Confirm The Outgoing Trust, and then click Next.

14. On the Confirm Incoming Trust page, select Yes, Confirm The Incoming Trust, and then click Next.

15. On the Completing The New Trust Wizard page (as shown in the following example from Computer03), click Finish.

16. Click OK in the Contoso*pp*.local Properties dialog box.

17. Close the Active Directory Domains And Trusts console.

Creating the SDP

The following steps will create a shared folder with the appropriate permissions for an SDP.

> **IMPORTANT**   Complete the following steps from the odd-numbered computers.

1. From the Start menu, point to Administrative Tools, and select Manage Your Server.

2. In the Manage Your Server window, if the File Server section is available, click Manage This File Server, and in the File Server Management console, in the scope pane, ensure that Shares (Local) is selected. From the Action menu, select New Share. Skip to step 9.

3. If the File Server section is not present, in the Manage Your Server window, click Add Or Remove A Role.

4. In the Configure Your Server Wizard, on the Preliminary Steps page, click Next.

5. On the Server Role page, select File Server, and click Next.

6. On the File Server Disk Quotas page, click Next.

7. On the File Server Indexing Service page, click Next.

8. On the Summary Of Selections page, click Next.

9. In the Share A Folder Wizard, on the Welcome To The Share A Folder Wizard page, click Next.

10. On the Folder Path page, in the Path text box, type **C:\Call Centers SDP**, as shown in the following example. Click Next.

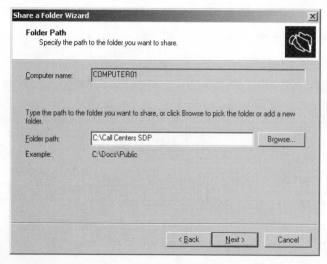

11. In the Share A Folder Wizard message box, click Yes to create the specified path.

12. On the Name, Description, And Settings page, click Next.

13. On the Permissions page, select Administrators Have Full Access; Other Users Have Read-Only Access, and then click Finish.

14. On the Sharing Was Successful page, click Close.

15. Copy the Proseware10.msi and Proseware25.msi files from C:\Lab Manual \Lab05 to the network share that you just created (\\Computer*pp* \Call Centers SDP).

16. Close all open windows.

EXERCISE 5-2: PUBLISHING SOFTWARE TO USERS THROUGH GROUP POLICY

Estimated completion time: 20 minutes

Management of the customer service call center at Contoso has asked you to allow users to install a new program from Proseware, Inc., that has proven useful to users in your partner domain (the Contoso*pp* domain with which you have created a two-way trust).

The call center employees all use Microsoft Windows XP Professional and are members of the Contoso*xx*.local domain. The software should be optional for all users in the Call Center *yy* Users security group to install through the Add And Remove Programs tool. The following steps accomplish this.

1. From the Start menu, point to Administrative Tools, and then select Group Policy Management.

2. In the Group Policy Management console, in the Scope pane, expand Forest: Contoso*xx*.local, expand Domains, expand Contoso*xx*.local, expand Call Centers, select and then right-click Call Center *yy*, and then select Create And Link A GPO Here, as shown in the following example from Computer04.

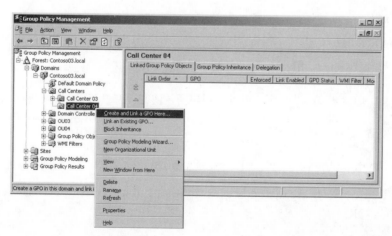

3. In the New GPO dialog box, in the Name text box, type **Call Center *yy* Software**, and press ENTER.

4. In the Group Policy Management console, in the details pane (press F5 to refresh if necessary), right-click the Call Center *yy* Software GPO, and then select Edit.

5. In the Group Policy Object Editor console, in the scope pane, under User Configuration, expand Software Settings, select and then right-click Software Installation, and then select Properties.

6. In the Software Installation Properties dialog box, in the General tab, click Browse.

7. In the Browse For Folder dialog box, browse to and select the shared folder created on Computer*pp* in the previous exercise (\\Computer*pp* \Call Centers SDP), as shown in the following example from Computer01 Click OK.

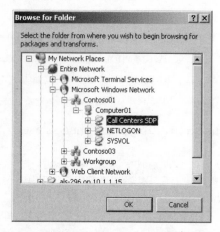

8. In the Software Installation Properties dialog box, in the Categories tab, click Add.

9. In the Enter New Category dialog box, type **Call Center *yy* Optional**, and then click OK.

10. In the Software Installation Properties dialog box, click OK.

11. In the Group Policy Object Editor, in the scope pane, ensure Software Installation is selected. From the Action menu, point to New, and then select Package.

12. In the Open dialog box, select Prosware10.msi, and then click Open.

13. In the Deploy Software dialog box, verify that Published is selected, and click OK.

14. In the Group Policy Object Editor console, in the details pane, right-click Proseware10, and select Properties.

15. In the Proseware10 Properties dialog box, in the Categories tab, in the Available Categories list box, ensure that Call Center *yy* Optional is selected, and then click Select, as shown in the following example. Click OK.

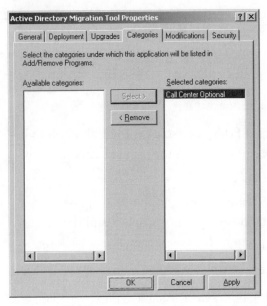

16. Log off and log on as JohnD if your computer number is odd, and JaneD if your computer number is even (leave the Password text box blank). When you log on, you will be asked to configure a new password (use the password P@ssw0rd, where the 0 character is a zero).

17. From the Start menu, select Control Panel.

18. In Control Panel, double-click Add Or Remove Programs.

19. In the Add Or Remove Programs window, click the Add New Programs icon on the left.

20. In the Add Programs From Your Network list box, click Add next to Proseware10.

21. In the Proseware10 message box confirming successful installation, click OK.

22. From the Start menu, point to All Programs, and select Proseware 1.0.

23. In the Windows Script Host message box, click OK to confirm that you have completed Exercise 5-2.

EXERCISE 5-3: ASSIGNING SOFTWARE TO USERS THROUGH GROUP POLICY

Estimated completion time: 5 minutes

The users that installed the optional program Proseware 1.0 have reported that it is very useful, and call center management has decided to make the software mandatory for all call center employees. You are going to assign the latest version, Proseware 2.5, to all users in the Call Center yy Users security group.

1. Log on with your Administrator account.

2. Open the Group Policy Object Editor console for the Call Center yy Software Group Policy Object (GPO) (use the same technique as in step 4 of the previous exercise).

3. In the Group Policy Object Editor console, in the scope pane, under User Configuration, expand Software Settings, select and then right-click Software Installation, point to New, and then select Package.

4. In the Open dialog box, select Proseware25.msi, and then click Open.

5. In the Deploy Software dialog box, select Assigned, and then click OK.

6. In the Group Policy Object Editor console, in the details pane, right-click Proseware25, and then select Properties.

7. In the Proseware25 Properties dialog box, in the Deployment tab, in the Deployment Options section, select the Install This Application At Logon check box.

8. In the Upgrades tab, click Add.

9. In the Add Upgrade Package, ensure that Current Group Policy Object (GPO) is selected, that Prosware10 is selected, and that Uninstall The Existing Package, Then Install The Upgrade Package is selected. Click OK.

10. In the Proseware25 Properties dialog box, in the Upgrades tab, select the Required Upgrade For Existing Packages check box, and then Click OK.

11. Log off and log back on as JohnD if your computer number is odd, and JaneD if your computer number is even.

12. From the Start menu, point to All Programs, and then select Proseware 2.5.

13. Click OK in the Windows Script Host message box to confirm that you have completed Exercise 5-3.

EXERCISE 5-4: REMOVING SOFTWARE THROUGH GROUP POLICY

Estimated completion time: 5 minutes

Management has decided to use a program from a different vendor to replace Proseware. You have been asked to configure Group Policy to remove Proseware 2.5.

1. Log on with your Administrator account.

2. Open the Group Policy Object Editor console for the Call Center *yy* Software GPO.

3. In the Group Policy Object Editor console, in the scope pane, under User Configuration, expand Software Settings, and select Software Installation.

4. In the details pane, right-click Proseware25, point to All Tasks, and select Remove.

5. In the Remove Software dialog box, verify that Immediately Uninstall The Software From Users And Computers is selected, as shown in the following example. Click OK.

6. Log off and log back on as JohnD if your computer number is odd, and JaneD if your computer number is even.

7. From the Start menu, point to All Programs. Note that Proseware 2.5 has been removed.

EXERCISE 5-5: RESTRICTING SOFTWARE THROUGH GROUP POLICY USING PATHS

Estimated completion time: 15 minutes

A previously friendly competition among the call center employees of writing insurance product haiku in Notepad has turned ugly. To ensure that morale slips no further, you have been asked to prevent the offending group from running Notepad.

1. Log on with your Administrator account.

2. Open the Group Policy Object Editor console for the Call Center *yy* Software GPO.

3. In the Group Policy Object Editor console, in the scope pane, under User Configuration, expand Windows Settings, expand Security Settings, and select Software Restriction Policies, as shown in the following example from Computer03.

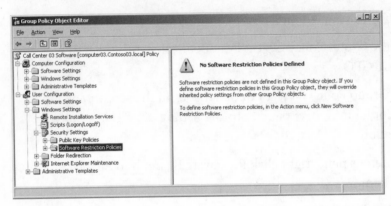

4. From the Action menu, select New Software Restriction Policies.

5. In the scope pane, expand Software Restriction Policies, select and then right-click Additional Rules, and then select New Path Rule.

6. In the New Path Rule dialog box, in the Path text box, type **%systemroot%\system32\notepad.exe**. In the Description text box, type **No more haiku**. Ensure that Disallowed is selected in the Security Level drop-down list. Click OK.

> **QUESTION** Why is it better to use %systemroot% rather than C:\WINDOWS in the path?

7. Log off and log back on as JohnD if your computer number is odd, and JaneD if your computer number is even.

8. From the Start menu, point to All Programs, point to Accessories, and select Notepad.

9. Read the message box, and click OK.

10. From the Start menu, select Run.

11. In the Run dialog box, in the Open text box, type **C:\Windows \Notepad.exe**, and press ENTER.

> **QUESTION** Why is Notepad allowed to open?

EXERCISE 5-6: RESTRICTING SOFTWARE THROUGH GROUP POLICY USING A HASH

Estimated completion time: 5 minutes

The call center employees circumvented the measures you took to prevent Notepad from running by invoking it from a different path, and haiku are now being written with irresponsible abandon. Morale has plunged to new lows, and the legal department is getting nervous. You have been asked to ensure that the felonious poets are not able to run Notepad, regardless of the path.

1. Log on with your Administrator account (the password is P@ssw0rd).

2. Open the Group Policy Object Editor console for the Call Center *yy* Software GPO.

3. In the Group Policy Object Editor console, in the scope pane, expand User Configuration, expand Windows Settings, expand Security Settings, expand Software Restriction Policies, select and then right-click Additional Rules, and then select New Hash Rule.

4. In the New Hash Rule dialog box, in the File Hash text box, click Browse.

5. In the Open dialog box, browse to C:\Windows\Notepad.exe, and click Open.

6. In the New Hash Rule dialog box, a long string of characters will appear in the File Hash text box. In the Description text box, type **NO MORE HAIKU!** Ensure that Disallowed is selected in the Security Level drop-down list (as shown in the following figure). Click OK.

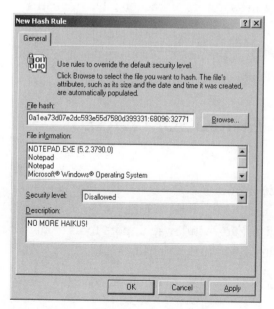

MORE INFO   *A hash is the result of a hash algorithm. A hash algorithm takes one string of characters (in this case from the file Notepad.exe) and creates another, usually shorter, string of characters based on the first string (called a hash). Hash algorithms are designed to distribute the set of results from different input strings as evenly and randomly as possible over the domain ("domain" here means the set of possible results of a function) to make it unlikely for two different input strings to create the same hash. However, duplications can occur (two different input strings can result in the same hash). Although the hash might look random, it isn't, because the result is reproducible given the same input string.*

7. Log off and log back on as JohnD if your computer number is odd, and JaneD if your computer number is even.

8. Open a Run dialog box, and in the Open text box, type **C:\Windows \Notepad.exe**, and then press ENTER.

9. Read the message box, and click OK.

LAB REVIEW QUESTIONS

Estimated completion time: 15 minutes

1. What is required in Windows Server 2003 for an SDP in forest A to be utilized by Group Policy in forest B?

2. What is the difference between assigning and publishing software to users through Group Policy?

3. What is the difference between assigning and publishing software to computers through Group Policy?

4. What is an easy way of negating software restrictions that use paths?

5. Given that restricting software access using a hash requires that the restricted hash match the hash of the program you invoke, how could a hacker cause a hash restriction to fail?

LAB CHALLENGE 5-1: ASSIGNING SOFTWARE TO COMPUTERS

Estimated completion time: 20 minutes

Currently, the servers in the domain do not have Windows Support Tools installed. You have decided to distribute Windows Support Tools to all domain controllers in the domain. To do this, you will

■ Create a new SDP called Contoso*xx* SDP on Computer*xx*.

- Copy SUPTOOLS.MSI and SUPPORT.CAB from the Windows Server 2003 installation CD to the new SDP.

- Configure a new GPO named Contoso*xx* DC Software to deploy the software.

- Verify the results.

> **IMPORTANT** Computer*xx* must remain on while the even-numbered computer restarts so that the SDP is available.

LAB CHALLENGE 5-2: UNDERSTANDING HOW HASH RESTRICTIONS WORK

Estimated completion time: 15 minutes

To investigate the effectiveness of software restrictions, you have been asked to demonstrate how a hacker might compromise software restriction policies based on a hash.

Do the following:

- Create a disallow software restriction for the Example.vbs file in C:\Lab Manual\Lab05 for users in the Call Center *yy* OU using a hash rule.

- Copy the Example.vbs file to Shared Documents.

- Verify that it won't run when invoked by users in the Call Center *yy* OU.

- Compromise the software restriction. (Hint: The ' character in a .vbs file means to ignore everything after it on that line.)

- Verify that the program will now run when invoked by a user in the Call Center *yy* OU.

MICROSOFT WINDOWS SERVER 2003 SECURITY CONFIGURATION

This lab contains the following exercises and activities:

■ Exercise 6-1: Configuring Audit Policy

■ Exercise 6-2: Configuring Security Options

■ Exercise 6-3: Configuring Restricted Groups

■ Exercise 6-4: Creating a Member Server Security Baseline

■ Lab Review Questions

■ Lab Challenge 6-1: Configuring Security for Role-Specific Servers

SCENARIO

Contoso is going to be deploying new security for specific groups and across the domain. To do so, you will need to revisit audit policy and security options. To prevent any intruders from escalating a normal account to an administrator level, you will implement restricted groups. Finally, you will devise a baseline security Group Policy Object (GPO) for all member servers in the domain.

After completing this lab, you will be able to:

- Configure auditing and use the Event Viewer console to view audits
- Configure security options
- Restrict group membership
- Create and apply a baseline security policy

Estimated completion time: 90 minutes

BEFORE YOU BEGIN

To complete this lab, you need to ensure that the following dependencies are completed:

- You must install the Group Policy Management Console (GPMC) using the Gpmc.msi installer package, if you did not do so in the Lab Challenge 4-1 for Lab 4, or the Before You Begin section in Lab 5. To install GPMC, run Gpmc.msi, which is located in the C:\Lab Manual \Lab04 folder, and follow the on-screen instructions.

- If you did not do so in the Before You Begin section of Lab 5, you need to run the ADUCUpdate*xx*.vbs file located in C:\Lab Manual\Lab05. This script will create the structure pictured in Figure 6-1.

In this lab, you'll need to pair with the student that is a member of the same domain as you, as established in Lab 1, "Reviewing Microsoft Active Directory Concepts."

This lab often refers to the number of your domain, your computer, or your partner's computer according to the following conventions:

- *xx* is the number of your domain.
- *yy* is the number of your computer.
- *zz* is the number of your partner's computer.

For example, if you are using Computer04, *xx* = 03 (you are a member of Contoso03.local), *yy* = 04 (you are using Computer04), and *zz* = 03 (your partner is using Computer03).

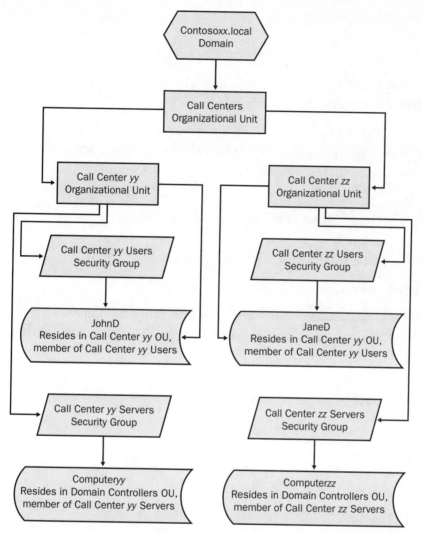

Figure 6-1   The ADUCUpdate*xx*.vbs script creates this structure within Active Directory

EXERCISE 6-1: CONFIGURING AUDIT POLICY

Estimated completion time: 20 minutes

You suspect that an employee is changing payroll data to defraud the company. To try to find out who is doing this, you need to implement the appropriate auditing. You suspect that the perpetrator is a member of the Administrators group.

> **NOTE**   This scenario presents a fairly naïve, though not necessarily unrealistic, attempt at breaching security. A more sophisticated hacker could use the powerful privileges of the Administrators group to cover tracks in a number of ways. The point of the exercise is not to demonstrate how a sophisticated hacker would breach security, but rather to demonstrate how to audit an object for a specific type of access, by a specific group, for security purposes.

IMPORTANT   *Complete steps 1 through 6 on the odd-numbered computer.*

1. Log on with your Administrator account (the password is P@ssw0rd).

2. From the Start menu, point to Administrative Tools, and then select Group Policy Management.

3. In the Group Policy Management console, expand Forest: Contosoxx .local, expand Domains, expand Contosoxx.local, expand Domain Controllers, select and then right-click Default Domain Controller Policy, and then select Edit.

4. In the Group Policy Object Editor console, in the scope pane, under Computer Configuration, expand Windows Settings, expand Security Settings, expand Local Policies, and select Audit Policy.

5. In the details pane, double-click Audit Object Access.

6. In the Audit Object Access Properties dialog box, select the Define These Policy Settings check box. Also select the Success check box. Click OK.

IMPORTANT   *Complete the remainder of the steps on both computers.*

7. From the Start menu, select Run.

8. In the Run dialog box, in the Open text box, type **gpupdate**, and press Enter.

9. Right-click the desktop, point to New, and then select Folder.

10. For the name of the folder, type **CC*yy* Employees**, and then press ENTER.

11. Right-click CC*yy* Employees, and select Properties.

12. In the CC*yy* Employees Properties dialog box, in the Security tab, click Advanced.

13. In the Advanced Security Settings For CC04 Employees dialog box, in the Auditing tab, click Add.

14. In the Select User, Computer, Or Group dialog box, in the Enter Object Name To Select (Examples) text box, type **Ad**, and then press ENTER.

15. In the Multiple Names Found dialog box, in the Matching Names list box, select Administrators, and then click OK.

16. In the Auditing Entry For CCyy Employees dialog box, in the Access list box, select the Successful check box for the Create Files / Write Data item, as shown in the following example. Click OK.

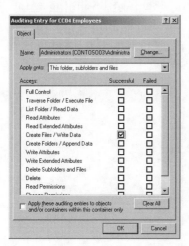

17. In the Advanced Security Settings For CCyy Employees dialog box, click OK.

18. In the CCyy Employees Properties dialog box, click OK.

19. Open the CCyy Employees folder.

20. In the CCyy Employees folder, from the File menu, point to New, and then select Text Document.

21. For the name of the text document, type **Payroll.txt**, and press ENTER.

22. Minimize the CCyy Employees folder.

23. From the Start menu, point to Administrative Tools, and select Event Viewer.

24. In the Event Viewer console, in the scope pane, select Security. From the Action menu, select Clear All Events.

25. In the Event Viewer message box, click No to indicate that you do not want to save before clearing.

26. Minimize Event Viewer.

27. Restore the CCyy Employees folder. Right-click the Payroll.txt file, point to Open With, and select WordPad.

28. In the Payroll.txt - WordPad document, type **Change**. From the File menu, select Exit.

29. In the WordPad message box, click Yes to save changes.

30. Restore the Event Viewer console, and press F5 to refresh the display.

31. Double-click the top event in the details pane.

32. In the Event Properties dialog box, click the downward-pointing arrow until you reach an event (as indicated in the Description scroll box) with an Object Name ending in Payroll.txt, as shown in the following example.

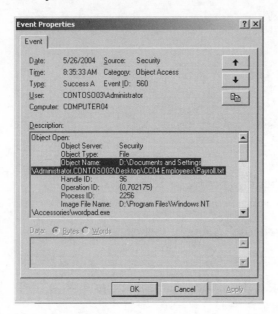

> **QUESTION**   What entry in the description of the event indicates that the Payroll.txt file was altered in WordPad?

> **QUESTION**   In this example, we limited auditing information to a member of the Administrators group and tracked only file creation and data writing. Why is it important to narrow your auditing parameters as much as possible?

33. Close all open windows except the Group Policy Management console, which is used by the odd-numbered computer in Exercise 6-3.

EXERCISE 6-2: CONFIGURING SECURITY OPTIONS

Estimated completion time: 5 minutes

The domain controllers are set to lock when the screen saver starts. This means that whenever you visit a domain controller that has been untouched for a while, it is locked, and you are unable to shut it down or restart it without logging on first. For convenience, you want to be able to shut down domain controllers when they are locked.

IMPORTANT   *Complete this exercise on the even-numbered computer.*

1. Open the Group Policy Management console. In the scope pane, expand Forest: Contoso*xx*, expand Domains, expand Contoso03.local, expand Domain Controllers, select Default Domain Controllers Policy, and from the Action menu, select Edit.

2. In the Group Policy Object Editor console, in the scope pane, under Computer Configuration, expand Windows Settings, expand Security Settings, expand Local Policies, and then select Security Options.

3. In the details pane, double-click Shutdown: Allow System To Be Shut Down Without Having To Log On.

4. In the Shutdown: Allow System To Be Shut Down Without Having To Log On Properties dialog box, select the Define This Setting check box, and verify Enabled is selected. Click OK.

5. Restart your computer and note that the Shut Down button in the Log On To Windows dialog box is active. Log on with your Administrator account.

EXERCISE 6-3: CONFIGURING RESTRICTED GROUPS

Estimated completion time: 15 minutes

To ensure that an intruder is unable to escalate a nonadministrator account to an administrator account (by joining the Administrators group), you need to restrict membership to the Administrators group.

Restricting the Administrators Group

The following steps will restrict membership to the Administrators group.

IMPORTANT   *Complete the following task on the odd-numbered computer only.*

1. In the Group Policy Management console, expand Forest, expand Domains, expand Contoso*xx*.local, select and then right-click Default Domain Policy, and then select Edit.

2. In the Group Policy Object Editor, in the scope pane, under Computer Configuration, expand Windows Settings, expand Security Settings, expand Local Policies, select and then right-click Restricted Groups, and then select Add Group.

3. In the Add Group dialog box, in the Group text box, browse to or type **Administrators**, and then click OK.

4. In the Administrators Properties dialog box, in the Members Of This Group section, click Add.

5. In the Add Member dialog box, in the Members Of This Group text box, browse to or type **Contosoxx\Administrator**. Click OK.

6. An example of the Administrators Properties dialog box configured correctly is shown in the following figure from Computer04. Click OK. Close the Group Policy Object Editor console, and leave the Group Policy Management console open for the next exercise.

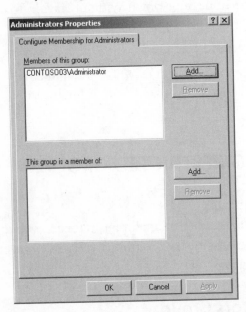

Testing the Restriction

In the following steps you will add a user to the Administrators group, which is restricted according to the Default Domain Controllers GPO that you just modified. You will then see that the restricted membership is removed from the Administrators group after Group Policy is refreshed.

IMPORTANT   *Complete the following steps on both computers.*

1. From the Start menu, point to Administrative Tools, and then select Active Directory Users And Computers.

2. In the Active Directory Users And Computers console, in the scope pane, expand Contosoyy.local, expand Call Centers, and then select Call Center yy.

3. In the details pane, select and then right-click JohnD if your computer name has an odd number, and JaneD if your computer name has an even number. Select Properties.

4. In the user Properties dialog box, in the Member Of tab, click Add.

5. In the Select Groups dialog box, in the Enter The Object Name To Select (Examples) text box, type **Ad**, and click Check Names. Administrators should appear underlined. Click OK.

6. An example of the Member Of tab of the user Properties dialog box from Computer04 is shown in the following example. Click OK.

7. Run Gpupdate from the Run dialog box.

> **IMPORTANT**   Wait until your partner has completed step 7 before continuing.

8. In the Active Directory Users And Computers console, navigate to the Member Of tab in the Properties dialog box for JohnD or JaneD, as appropriate.

> **QUESTION**   Is the user a member of the Administrators group? Why?

EXERCISE 6-4: CREATING A MEMBER SERVER SECURITY BASELINE

Estimated completion time: 35 minutes

To tighten security across all member servers in the domain, you are going to "harden" the security policies for member servers. Eventually, this will require fully defining a GPO attached to an organizational unit (OU) containing all member servers. For the time being, you are just going to configure the baseline System Services for member servers.

1. In the Group Policy Management console, in the scope pane, expand Forest: Contosoxx.local, expand Domains, and select Contosoxx.local.

2. From the Action menu, select New Organizational Unit.

3. In the New Organizational Unit dialog box, in the Name text box, type **Member Servers**, and press ENTER.

4. Create and link a GPO called Member Server Baseline to the Member Servers OU according to the technique described in Lab Exercise 5-2, "Publishing Software to Users Through Group Policy," steps 1 through 3.

5. Open the Group Policy Object Editor console for the Member Server Baseline GPO.

6. In the Group Policy Object Editor console, in the scope pane, under Computer Configuration, expand Windows Settings, expand Security Settings, and select System Services.

7. In the details pane, double-click Alerter, select the Define This Policy Setting check box, and ensure that Disabled is selected. Click OK.

8. For each service, define the policy setting according to Table 6-1.

> **IMPORTANT**   Table 6-1 might vary from the options that you have depending on your configuration and which lab exercises you have completed. Ignore differences and configure the policies as closely as possible.

Table 6-1   Baseline Settings for System Services

Policy	Setting
Alerter	Disabled
Application Layer Gateway Service	Disabled
Application Management	Disabled
Automatic Updates	Automatic
Background Intelligent Transfer Service	Manual

Table 6-1   **Baseline Settings for System Services (Continued)**

Policy	Setting
ClipBook	Disabled
COM+ Event System	Manual
COM+ System Application	Disabled
Computer Browser	Automatic
Cryptographic Services	Automatic
DHCP Client	Automatic
Distributed File System	Disabled
Distributed Link Tracking Client	Disabled
Distributed Link Tracking Server	Disabled
Distributed Transaction Coordinator	Disabled
DNS Client	Automatic
DNS Server	Disabled
Error Reporting Service	Disabled
Event Log	Automatic
File Replication Service	Disabled
Help And Support	Disabled
HTTP SSL	Disabled
Human Interface Device Access	Disabled
IMAPI CD-Burning COM Service	Disabled
Indexing Service	Disabled
Internet Connection Firewall (ICF)/Internet Connection Sharing (ICS)	Disabled
Intersite Messaging	Disabled
IPSEC Services	Automatic
Kerberos Key Distribution Center	Disabled
License Logging	Disabled
Logical Disk Manager	Manual
Logical Disk Manager Administrative Service	Manual
Messenger	Disabled
Microsoft Software Shadow Copy Provider	Disabled
Net Logon	Automatic
NetMeeting Remote Desktop Sharing	Disabled
Network Connections	Manual
Network DDE	Disabled
Network DDE DSDM	Disabled
Network Location Awareness	Manual
NT LM Security Support Provider	Automatic

Table 6-1   Baseline Settings for System Services (Continued)

Policy	Setting
Performance Logs And Alerts	Manual
Plug And Play	Automatic
Portable Media Serial Number Service	Disabled
Print Spooler	Disabled
Protected Storage	Automatic
Remote Access Auto Connection Manager	Disabled
Remote Access Connection Manager	Disabled
Remote Desktop Help Session Manager	Disabled
Remote Procedure Call (RPC)	Automatic
Remote Procedure Call (RPC) Locator	Disabled
Remote Registry	Automatic
Removable Storage	Disabled
Resultant Set Of Policy Provider	Disabled
Routing And Remote Access	Disabled
Secondary Logon	Disabled
Security Accounts Manager	Automatic
Server	Automatic
Shell Hardware Detection	Disabled
Smart Card	Disabled
Special Administration Console Helper	Disabled
System Event Notification	Automatic
Task Scheduler	Disabled
TCP/IP NetBIOS Helper	Automatic
Telephony	Disabled
Telnet	Disabled
Terminal Services	Automatic
Terminal Services Session Directory	Disabled
Themes	Disabled
Uninterruptible Power Supply	Disabled
Upload Manager	Disabled
Virtual Disk Service	Disabled
Volume Shadow Copy	Manual
WebClient	Disabled
Windows Audio	Disabled
Windows Image Acquisition	Disabled
Windows Installer	Automatic
Windows Management Instrumentation	Automatic

Table 6-1   **Baseline Settings for System Services (Continued)**

Policy	Setting
Windows Management Instrumentation Driver Extensions	Manual
Windows Time	Automatic
WinHTTP Web Proxy Auto-Discovery Service	Disabled
Wireless Configuration	Disabled
WMI Performance Adapter	Manual
Workstation	Automatic

LAB REVIEW QUESTIONS

Estimated completion time: 15 minutes

1. When defining the policy settings through the Properties dialog box of an audit policy, there are four possible configurations. What are they?

2. What tool is used to view the results of auditing?

3. Configuring Audit Object Access is only half of auditing the access of an object. What else must be configured before an object will be audited?

4. Two things are accomplished when you list a member when restricting membership to a group through Restricted Groups. The first is that that member will not be removed from the group when the policy refreshes. What is the second?

5. After creating a baseline GPO and OU for member servers, you want to create an OU and GPO for print servers. Only a few policies for the print servers are different than those of the member servers. Where is the logical place to locate the OU and GPO for the print servers?

LAB CHALLENGE 6-1: CONFIGURING SECURITY FOR ROLE-SPECIFIC SERVERS

Estimated completion time: 30 minutes

Having configured baseline security for member servers, you need to create OUs within the Member Servers OU and link new GPOs to these new OUs to handle the security settings for servers with the following roles: Infrastructure Servers (servers that run Dynamic Host Configuration Protocol [DHCP] or Windows Internet Naming Service [WINS]), File Servers, and Print Servers. For now, you are going to configure only System Services for each role. Because you have already defined a baseline, all you need to do in each GPO is modify the settings where appropriate. To complete the challenge, do the following:

1. Create OUs under the Member Servers OU configured in Exercise 6-4, "Creating a Member Server Security Baseline." Call the new OUs Infrastructure Servers, File Servers, and Print Servers.

2. Create three GPOs attached one each to the new OUs, and call them Infrastructure Servers Security, File Servers Security, and Print Servers Security, respectively.

3. Configure the System Services settings according to the roles that the servers will be filling. As a guide, consult the following resources (each is a chapter in the *Windows Server 2003 Security Guide*, provided by Microsoft TechNet):

   - *http://www.microsoft.com/technet/Security/prodtech/win2003 /w2003hg/sgch05.mspx*

   - *http://www.microsoft.com/technet/Security/prodtech/win2003 /w2003hg/sgch06.mspx*

   - *http://www.microsoft.com/technet/Security/prodtech/win2003 /w2003hg/sgch07.mspx*

LAB 7
SECURITY TEMPLATES

This lab contains the following exercises and activities:

■ Exercise 7-1: Examining Security Templates

■ Exercise 7-2: Creating and Editing a Security Template

■ Exercise 7-3: Using the Security Configuration And Analysis Tool for Analysis

■ Exercise 7-4: Using Secedit to Create a Rollback Template

■ Exercise 7-5: Using the Security Configuration And Analysis Tool for Configuration

■ Exercise 7-6: Using Secedit

■ Exercise 7-7: Deploying a Security Template Through a Group Policy Object

■ Lab Review Questions

■ Lab Challenge 7-1: Creating a Security Template Using Notepad

■ Lab Challenge 7-2: Scripting Secedit

SCENARIO

You have been asked to increase and standardize security across computers with similar roles. You have decided that security templates applied through Group Policy are the best way to accomplish this.

In preparation for launching a pilot run of new security templates, you are creating and testing the new templates on a test system. Included in your testing will be the creating of a template by copying a built-in template, editing a template using the Security Templates snap-in, and analysis and configuration of templates using the Security Configuration And Analysis snap-in. Also, you want to generate a rollback template so that you can undo changes if need be. Finally, in some cases you may only want to apply parts of a template, so you need to test partial deployment of a security template using Secedit.

After completing this lab, you will be able to:

- Use the Security Templates snap-in.

- Use the Security Configuration And Analysis snap-in.

- Deploy security templates through various methods.

- Use the Secedit command-line utility.

Estimated completion time: 85 minutes

BEFORE YOU BEGIN

To complete this lab, you need to ensure that the following dependencies are completed.

- You must install the Group Policy Management Console (GPMC) using the Gpmc.msi installer package, if you did not do so in the Lab Challenge 4-1 for Lab 4, "Group Policy Strategy," or the "Before You Begin" section in Lab 5, "Managing the User and Computer Environment with Group Policy," or Lab 6, "Microsoft Windows Server 2003 Security Configuration." To install GPMC, run Gpmc.msi, which is located in the C:\Lab Manual\Lab04 folder, and follow the on-screen instructions.

- If you did not do so in the Before You Begin section of Lab 5 or 6, you need to run the ADUCUpdate*xx*.vbs file located in C:\Lab Manual \Lab05. This script will create the structure pictured in Figure 7-1.

This lab often refers to the number of your domain and your computer according to the following conventions:

- *xx* is the number of your domain.

- *yy* is the number of your computer.

For example, if you are using Computer04, *xx* = 03 (you are a member of Contoso03.local), and *yy* = 04 (you are using Computer04).

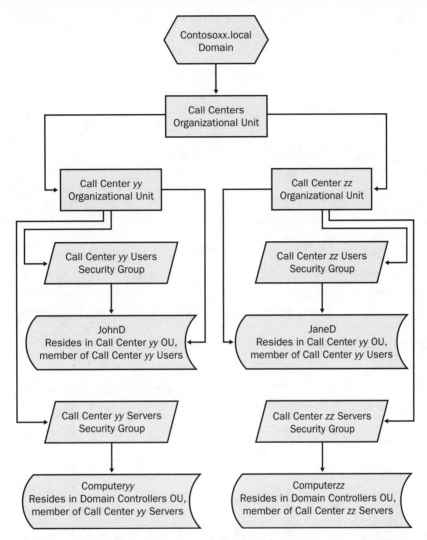

Figure 7-1   The ADUCUpdate*xx*.vbs script creates this structure within Active Directory

EXERCISE 7-1: EXAMINING SECURITY TEMPLATES

Estimated completion time: 20 minutes

To become familiar with the contents of security templates and how they are represented in the Security Templates snap-in, you will examine a security template both in Notepad and in the Security Templates snap-in.

Examining Security Templates Using the Security Template Snap-In

The following steps create a console with the Security Templates snap-in added. You can then use the snap-in to examine a security template.

1. Log on with your Administrator account (the password is **P@ssw0rd**).

2. From the Start menu, select Run.

3. In the Run dialog box, in the Open text box, type **mmc**, and then press ENTER.

4. In the Console1 console, from the File menu, select Add/Remove Snap-In.

5. In the Add/Remove Snap-In dialog box, in the Standalone tab, click Add.

6. In the Add Standalone Snap-In dialog box, in the Available Standalone Snap-Ins list box, select Security Templates, and then click Add. Click Close.

7. In the Add/Remove Snap-In dialog box, click OK.

8. In the Console1 console, in the scope pane, expand Security Templates, expand C:\Windows\Security\Templates, expand Compatws, and select Restricted Groups, as shown in the following example.

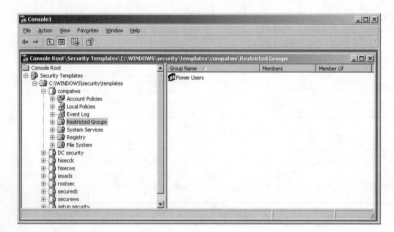

> **QUESTION**   Users belonging to which built-in security group will be removed from that group if the Compatws security template is applied to a workstation?

9. Examine the Rootsec template node.

> **QUESTION**   What is the only node within the Rootsec subtree that has policies defined?

10. Examine the Setup Security template node.

> **QUESTION**   In the Setup Security template, who is allowed the user right Take Ownership Of Files Or Other Objects?

11. From the File menu, select Save As.

12. In the Save As dialog box, click the Desktop icon on the left, and save the console as **Security Templates**.

13. Leave the Security Templates console open for the next exercise.

Examining Security Templates Using Notepad

The following steps will examine the Hisecdc security template using Notepad.

1. From the Start menu, point to All Programs, point to Accessories, and select Notepad.

2. In Notepad, from the File menu, select Open.

3. In the Open dialog box, in the Look In drop-down list, browse to C:\Windows\Security\Templates.

4. In the File Name text box, type *.* and then press ENTER.

5. Select the Hisecdc.inf file, and click Open. The file is shown in Notepad in the following figure.

> **QUESTION**   What Lockout policies are set in the Hisecdc security template (answer with the policy names as they appear in the graphical user interface [GUI], not as they appear in the .inf file), and what are the values?

6. Open the Compatws.inf file in Notepad.

> **QUESTION**   Which policy group has more configuration entries in the Compatws security template than any other by a large margin?

7. Close Notepad.

EXERCISE 7-2: CREATING AND EDITING A SECURITY TEMPLATE

Estimated completion time: 10 minutes

To begin testing for your pilot run, you need to create a template. The following exercise copies an existing template and uses the Security Templates snap-in to edit it. The template needs to be edited to enable the Removable Storage service with access granted only to System, which is a necessary configuration for a proprietary backup system that Contoso uses for sensitive data.

1. Create a folder named **Custom** in C:\Windows\Security\Templates.

2. Copy the Securedc.inf file from C:\Windows\Security\Templates to the Custom folder.

3. Rename the Securedc.inf file in the Custom folder to CallCenters.inf.

4. In the Security Templates console, in the scope pane, select Security Templates.

5. From the Action menu, select New Template Search Path.

6. In the Browse For Folder dialog box, browse to the Custom folder you just created, and click OK.

7. In the Security Templates console, in the scope pane, expand C:\Windows\Security\Templates\Custom, expand CallCenters, and then select System Services, as shown in the following example.

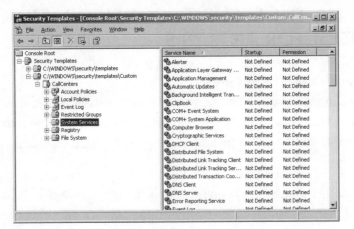

8. In the Details pane, double-click Removable Storage.

9. In the Removable Storage Properties dialog box, select the Define This Policy Setting In The Template check box, and then select Automatic. Click Edit Security.

10. In the Security For Removable Storage dialog box, in the Group Or User Names list box, remove all entries except SYSTEM, as shown in the following example, and then click OK.

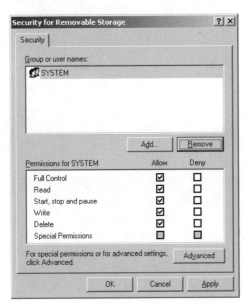

11. In the Removable Storage Properties dialog box, click OK.

12. In the Security Templates console, in the scope pane, select Call-Centers. From the Action menu, select Save.

13. Leave the Security Templates console open for the next exercise.

EXERCISE 7-3: USING THE SECURITY CONFIGURATION AND ANALYSIS TOOL FOR ANALYSIS

Estimated completion time: 15 minutes

Now that you have a new security template, you want to compare its security settings with those of the system to which it will be applied. This will give you a warning of any possible conflicts that installing the new template may cause.

To determine how much your computer's security differs from a security template (or combination of security templates) you must first create a database to contain the template(s) and then use the Security Configuration And Analysis snap-in.

1. Add the Security Configuration And Analysis snap-in to the Security Templates console (use the same technique as described in steps 4 through 7 in the "Examining Security Templates Using the Security Template Snap-In" task of Exercise 7-1, "Examining Security Templates").

2. In the Security Templates console, in the scope pane, select Security Configuration And Analysis, and from the Action menu, select Open Database.

3. In the Open Database dialog box, in the File Name text box, type **CallCenterSecDB**, and click Open.

4. In the Import Template dialog box, select Hisecdc.inf, and then click Open (the Hisecdc.inf file resides in C:\Windows\Security\Templates).

5. In the Security Templates console, in the scope pane, select and right-click Security Configuration And Analysis, and then select Analyze Computer Now.

6. In the Perform Analysis dialog box, click OK to accept the default path for the error log file. An Analyzing System Security status box will appear while your system is analyzed. Wait for the analysis to finish before moving to the next step.

7. In the scope pane, expand Security Configuration And Analysis, expand Local Policies, and then select Audit Policy, as shown in the following figure.

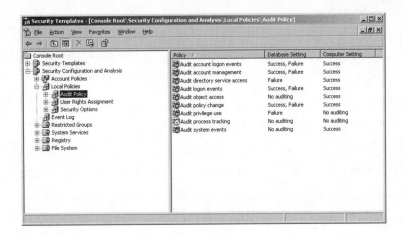

QUESTION   In the details pane, what does the red X flag on the Audit Account Logon Events policy icon denote?

8. In the scope pane, select Security Options.

QUESTION   In the details pane, what does the green check mark flag on the Accounts: Guest Account Status policy icon denote?

9. In the scope pane, select System Services.

QUESTION   Is there a flag on the Removable Storage service? If so, describe it.

10. In the scope pane, select and then right-click Security Configuration And Analysis, and then select Import Template.

11. In the Import Template dialog box, navigate to C:\Windows\Security \Templates\Custom, and select CallCenters.inf. Click Open.

12. From the Action menu, select Analyze Computer Now. An Analyzing System Security status box will appear while your system is analyzed. Wait for the analysis to finish before moving to the next step.

13. In the Perform Analysis dialog box, click OK to accept the default path for the error log.

14. Navigate to System Services under the Security Configuration And Analysis node.

QUESTION   What flag marks the Removable Storage service now?

15. In the Security Templates console, in the scope pane, select and then right-click Security Configuration And Analysis, and then select Export Template.

16. In the Export Template dialog box, select CallCenters.inf, and then click Save.

17. In the Security Templates console, from the File menu, select Save.

18. Leave the Security Templates window open for Exercise 7-5, "Using the Security Configuration And Analysis Tool for Configuration."

EXERCISE 7-4: USING SECEDIT TO CREATE A ROLLBACK TEMPLATE

Estimated completion time: 5 minutes

You want to test the new template that you have created, but first you will create a rollback template that will allow you to restore the original security settings on your computer.

1. Open a Run dialog box. In the Open text box, type **cmd**, and then press ENTER.

2. At the command prompt, change the directory to C:\Windows\Security \Templates\Custom.

3. At the command prompt, type **secedit /generaterollback /cfg CallCenters.inf /rbk Rollback1.inf**, and then press ENTER.

4. Press Y, and then press ENTER to confirm that you would like to continue the operation. Example results are shown in the following figure.

5. Leave the command prompt window open for Exercise 7-6, "Using Secedit."

EXERCISE 7-5: USING THE SECURITY CONFIGURATION AND ANALYSIS TOOL FOR CONFIGURATION

Estimated completion time: 5 minutes

To deploy your new template on the local machine, you will use the Security Configuration And Analysis snap-in.

1. In the Security Templates console, in the scope pane, select and then right-click Security Configuration And Analysis, and then select Configure Computer Now.

2. In the Configure System dialog box, click OK to accept the default path for the error log.

3. In the Security Templates console, in the scope pane, select and right-click Security Configuration And Analysis, and then select Analyze Computer Now. An Analyzing System Security status box will appear while your system is analyzed. Wait for the analysis to finish before moving to the next step.

4. In the Perform Analysis dialog box, click OK to accept the default path for the error log.

5. In the scope pane, expand Security Configuration And Analysis, expand Local Policies, and then select Audit Policy.

> **QUESTION** In the details pane, why is there no longer a red X flag on the Audit Account Logon Events policy icon?

6. Close the Security Templates console. In the Microsoft Management Console message box asking if you want to save changes, click Yes.

EXERCISE 7-6: USING SECEDIT

Estimated completion time: 10 minutes

Having tested the new security template, you want to return to the original security settings. To do this, you will use Secedit. After that, you want to apply just the registry key changes as a test. Finally, you anticipate that you might edit some security templates by hand, and you want to learn how to validate them using Secedit.

Using Secedit to Roll Back to a Previous Configuration

The following steps will restore the previous security configuration.

1. In the command prompt window, change the directory to
   C:\Windows\Security\Templates\Custom.

2. At the command prompt, type **secedit /configure /db temp.sdb /cfg
   Rollback1.inf**, and then press ENTER. An example is shown in the
   following figure.

Using Secedit to Partially Apply a Security Template

The following steps will apply only part of the CallCenters.inf template.

1. At the command prompt, type **secedit /configure /db temp.sdb /cfg
   CallCenters.inf /overwrite .inf /overwrite /areas regkeys**, and then
   press ENTER.

2. Press Y, and then press ENTER to answer yes when asked if you want to
   continue the operation.

> **QUESTION**   Why is the overwrite switch necessary?

Using Secedit to Validate a Template File

You have received a security template from a technician that was modified by
hand. In order to make sure that the syntax of the template is valid, you need to
check it with Secedit. Secedit can analyze a template file and report if there is
anything in it that will not be understood when it is applied. In order to see
Secedit do this, you will first create an error in a template.

1. Using Notepad, open the C:\Windows\Security\Templates\Custom
   \CallCenters.inf file.

2. In the [System Access] section, in a new first line, type **This will cause an error = 1**, and press ENTER. From the File menu, select Save As.

3. In the Save As dialog box, in the File Name text box, type **Example.inf**, and press ENTER. Close Notepad.

4. At the command prompt, type **secedit /validate Example.inf**, and then press ENTER.

QUESTION What problem did Secedit report?

5. Close the command prompt window and the Security Templates console.

EXERCISE 7-7: DEPLOYING A SECURITY TEMPLATE THROUGH A GROUP POLICY OBJECT

Estimated completion time: 5 minutes

Having finally experimented with templates enough to feel confident about running a pilot group as a test, you decide to use the CallCenter *yy* organizational unit (OU) as a test group because it is a small group with experienced users.

NOTE It would be useful if you could observe the changes that the security template applies in the following steps. Unfortunately, the only computer that is in the OU is your DC, and the settings will not be applied to your computer because policy assigned in the DC OU will trump these settings.

1. From the Start menu, point to Administrative Tools, and then select Group Policy Management.

2. In the Group Policy Management console, in the scope pane, expand Forests: Contoso*xx*.local, expand Contoso*xx*.local, expand Call Centers, expand Call Center *yy*, and then select CC*yy* Server Security.

3. From the Action menu, select Edit.

4. In the Group Policy Object Editor console, under Computer Configuration, expand Windows Settings, and then select Security Settings.

5. From the Action menu, select Import Policy.

6. In the Import Policy From dialog box, select CallCenters.inf, and click Open.

QUESTION What will this do?

7. Close the Group Policy Object Editor.

8. Close the Group Policy Management console.

LAB REVIEW QUESTIONS

Estimated completion time: 15 minutes

1. In which type of file are security templates stored?

2. When importing multiple templates into a database, how are conflicts resolved?

3. What are the four flags that are possible when using the Security Configuration And Analysis snap-in, and what do they denote?

4. For which two types of security is the Generaterollback parameter in Secedit unable to account?

5. The Secedit command and the Security Configuration And Analysis snap-in are good for applying security templates to single computers. What is an effective method of applying a template to many computers?

LAB CHALLENGE 7-1: CREATING A SECURITY TEMPLATE USING NOTEPAD

Estimated completion time: 20 minutes

To better understand the syntax of a security template file, create a security template in Notepad that configures the following (use an existing template as a base):

- Enforce password history for three passwords remembered

- Minimum password length of five characters

- Audit privilege use for failure

- Allow force shutdown for a remote system for administrators

- Allow add workstations to domain for authenticated users

Once you have completed the template file, save it as Challenge.inf in the C:\Windows\Security\Templates\Custom folder. Use Secedit to validate the file. Finally, ensure that the settings are as they should be by using the Security Templates console you created in Exercise 7-1.

LAB CHALLENGE 7-2: SCRIPTING SECEDIT

Estimated completion time: 10 minutes

Create and run a batch file that uses Secedit to do the following:

1. Validate the Challenge.inf template created in Lab Challenge 7-1, "Creating a Security Template Using Notepad."

2. Create a rollback based on the current security configuration and the Challenge.inf template.

3. Configure your machine with the User Rights policies from the Challenge.inf template, but make no other changes.

4. Configure your computer with the rollback template created in step 2.

5. Call the batch file **SeceditScript.bat.** Use **Temp.sdb** as the database name and **Rollback2.inf** as the rollback template name.

LAB 8

ADMINISTERING SOFTWARE UPDATE SERVICES

This lab contains the following exercises and activities:

- Exercise 8-1: Installing Software Update Services

- Exercise 8-2: Synchronizing Software Update Services with a Windows Update Server

- Exercise 8-3: Synchronizing Software Update Services with a Local SUS Server

- Exercise 8-4: Configuring the Automatic Updates Client Through Group Policy

- Exercise 8-5: Monitoring Software Update Services

- Lab Cleanup

- Lab Review Questions

- Lab Challenge 8-1: Configuring Windows Update Through Registry Settings

- Lab Challenge 8-2: Backing Up Software Update Services

SCENARIO

Currently, all servers within your domain are configured to download Windows updates from Windows Update servers directly. This has proved to be problematic for several reasons. First, the updates are not screened for possible problems they might cause critical applications. Second, having each machine access the Windows Update servers over the Internet causes excess Internet traffic.

To more tightly control which updates are applied, and to reduce traffic to the Windows Update servers, you are going to configure two SUS servers. One server will serve as the parent SUS server, and therefore communicate with the Windows

Update servers directly. The parent SUS server will be responsible for updating about half the computers at Contoso and will also synchronize with a child SUS server. The child SUS server will update the remainder of the computers at Contoso.

> **NOTE**   In this lab, you will pair with another domain. The odd-numbered computer in the lower-numbered domain will be configured as a parent SUS server, and the odd-numbered computer in the higher-numbered domain will be configured as its child. The two even-numbered computers will serve as SUS clients.

After completing this lab, you will be able to:

- Install and configure a Microsoft Software Update Services (SUS) server
- Synchronize SUS and approve updates
- Configure Automatic Updates through Group Policy and the Registry Editor
- Back up SUS metadata

Estimated completion time: 105 minutes

BEFORE YOU BEGIN

To complete this lab, you need to ensure that the following dependency completed:

- You must install the Group Policy Management Console (GPMC) using the Gpmc.msi (4.77 megabytes) installer package, if you did not do so in the Lab Challenge 4-1 for Lab 4, "Group Policy Strategy," or the "Before You Begin" sections of Lab 5, "Software Deployment and Restrictions Using Group Policy," Lab 6, "Microsoft Windows Server 2003 Security Configuration," or Lab 7, "Security Templates." To install GPMC, run GPMC.msi, which is located on the Student CD in the C:\Lab Manual\Lab04 folder, and follow the on-screen instructions.

In this lab, you'll need to pair with the student that is a member of the same domain as you, as established in Lab 1, "Reviewing Microsoft Active Directory Concepts."

This lab often refers to the number of your domain, your computer, or your partner's computer according to the following conventions:

- *xx* is the number of your domain.
- *yy* is the number of your computer.
- *zz* is the number of your partner's computer.

For example, if you are using Computer04, xx = 03 (you are a member of Contoso03.local), yy = 04 (you are using Computer04), and zz = 03 (your partner is using Computer03).

In addition, you are required to form a group with another domain, so that the group contains four computers in two domains. The number of the other domain is referred to as pp. For example, if you are a member of Contoso01.local and you pair with Contoso03.local, pp = 03.

EXERCISE 8-1: INSTALLING SOFTWARE UPDATE SERVICES

Estimated completion time: 15 minutes

To install SUS server, you must first install some components of the Microsoft Internet Information Services (IIS), which SUS requires to serve updates to SUS clients through Automatic Updates and to store the metadata, which is the configuration information and information about the updates (metadata means data about the data). After IIS is installed, SUS can be installed.

> **IMPORTANT**   Complete this exercise on the odd-numbered computers only. Ensure that your Microsoft Windows Server 2003 distribution CD is in your CD/DVD drive. If the Welcome To Microsoft Windows Server 2003 screen opens after you insert the CD, close it.

Installing IIS Components

The following steps will install components of IIS. You can see which components are being installed by viewing the details of the Internet Information Services (IIS) option before step 7.

1. Log on with the default Administrator account (the password is **P@ssw0rd**).

2. Copy the SUS installation file (SUS10SP1.exe) from the network share provided by your instructor, or download it to your desktop from *http://www.microsoft.com/windowsserversystem/sus/default.mspx* (32.2 megabytes).

3. From the Start menu, point to Control Panel, and select Add Or Remove Programs.

4. In the Add Or Remove Programs dialog box, click the Add/Remove Windows Components icon on the left.

5. In the Windows Components Wizard, on the Windows Components page, select Application Server (but do not select the check box next to it) as shown in the following example, and then click Details.

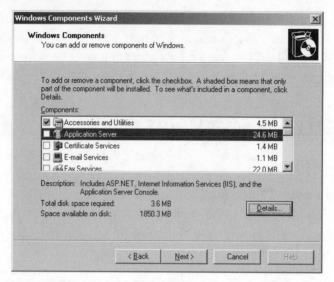

6. In the Application Server dialog box, in the Subcomponents Of Application Server list box, select the Internet Information Services (IIS) check box, and click OK.

> **NOTE** The Internet Information Services (IIS) component check box will have a shaded background with a black check mark. This happens because not all of the subcomponents are selected, which is okay. The Enable Network COM+ Access component is automatically selected when you select to install IIS, which is also okay.

7. In the Windows Components Wizard, on the Windows Components page, click Next.

8. The Configuring Components page will display progress during installation. The Completing The Windows Components Wizard page appears after installation. Click Finish.

9. Close the Add Or Remove Programs dialog box.

Installing the SUS Server

The following steps will install the SUS server. The default setup is as a parent. The SUS child server will be configured as such in a later exercise.

1. On your desktop, double-click SUS10SP1.exe (the SUS installation file).

2. In the Microsoft Software Update Services Wizard, on the Welcome To The Microsoft Software Update Services Wizard page, click Next.

3. On the End-User License Agreement page, select I Accept The Terms In The License Agreement, and then click Next.

4. On the Choose Setup Type page, click Custom.

> **NOTE** By selecting Custom, you are able to choose English Only on the next page of the wizard. This eliminates updates in other languages and thus saves time when synchronizing.

5. On the Choose File Locations page, click Next (leaving the default options configured).

6. On the Language Settings page, select English Only, and click Next.

7. On the Handling New Versions Of Previously Approved Updates page, verify that I Will Manually Approve New Versions Of Approved Updates is selected, and then click Next.

8. On the Ready To Install page, click Install.

9. The Installing Microsoft Software Update Services page will indicate progress. After installation, on the Completing The Microsoft Software Update Services Setup Wizard page, click Finish.

10. Microsoft Internet Explorer will open at the *http://localhost/SUSAdmin* location. An Internet Explorer dialog box might appear warning you about the Internet Explorer Enhanced Security Configuration. If you see this dialog box, click OK. Leave Internet Explorer open for the next exercise.

EXERCISE 8-2: SYNCHRONIZING SOFTWARE UPDATE SERVICES WITH A WINDOWS UPDATE SERVER

Estimated completion time: 60 minutes

For your parent SUS server to supply updates to SUS clients, including child SUS servers, it must first obtain the updates from the Windows Update servers. Therefore, you must synchronize the parent SUS server with the Windows Update servers. Also, to ensure that the SUS server remains up-to-date, you must schedule it to synchronize on a regular schedule (3 A.M. every day).

> **IMPORTANT** The following exercise requires Internet access. Complete the following task on the odd-numbered computer in the lower-numbered domain only.

1. In Internet Explorer, on the Welcome page of the Software Update Services site, in the navigation pane, click Synchronize Server.

2. On the Synchronize Server page, click Synchronization Schedule.

3. In the Schedule Synchronization—Web Page Dialog dialog box, select Synchronize Using This Schedule. In the At This Time drop-down list, ensure that 03:00 is selected, as shown in the following example. Click OK. Note that the next synchronization date and time is displayed.

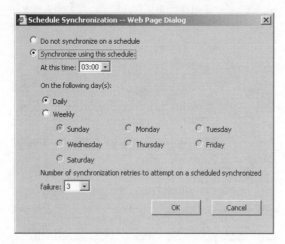

4. On the Synchronize Server page, click Synchronize Now.

5. The Synchronize Server page indicates the progress of the download. This could take 30 minutes or more depending on the speed of your Internet connection and the number of updates available.

> **IMPORTANT**   While step 5 is being completed, the SUS server on the odd-numbered computer in the higher-numbered domain can be configured (Exercise 8-3) and so can the SUS clients on both even-numbered computers (Exercise 8-4).

EXERCISE 8-3: SYNCHRONIZING SOFTWARE UPDATE SERVICES WITH A LOCAL SUS SERVER

Estimated completion time: 30 minutes

Now that the parent SUS server has received updates from the Windows Update servers, you must synchronize your child SUS server with its parent. The following steps identify the odd-numbered computer in the lower-numbered domain as the parent server.

> **IMPORTANT**   Complete the following task on the odd-numbered computer in the higher-numbered domain only.

1. In Internet Explorer, on the Welcome page of the Software Update Services site, in the navigation pane, click Set Options.

2. On the Set Options page, in the Select Which Server To Synchronize Content From section (you might need to scroll down to find this option), select Synchronize From A Local Software Update Server, and in the accompanying text box, type **http://computer***pp*. Select the Synchronize List Of Approved Items Updated From This Location (Replace Mode) check box, as shown in the following example from Computer03. Click Apply.

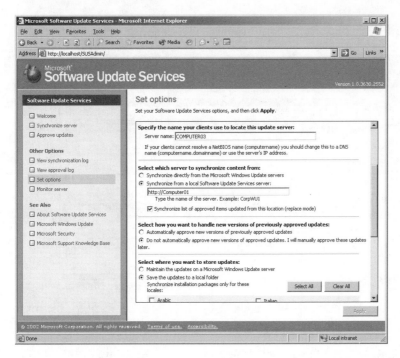

QUESTION   Selecting this option creates which type of topology between the SUS servers?

3. In the VBScript message box telling you that Microsoft recommends that you synchronize your server, click OK.

IMPORTANT   Wait until Exercise 8-2 on Computer*pp* is completed before continuing with step 4.

4. In the Software Update Services pane, on the left, click Synchronize Server.

5. On the Synchronize Server page, click Synchronize Now, if synchronization does not start automatically.

6. The Synchronize Server page will appear and indicate synchronization progress. This process could take several minutes or more depending on the speed of your network and the amount of updates to synchronize.

7. Click OK in the message box indicating that you have synchronized successfully.

8. On the Approve Updates page, select three of the smallest updates available, and click Approve. An example is shown in the following figure.

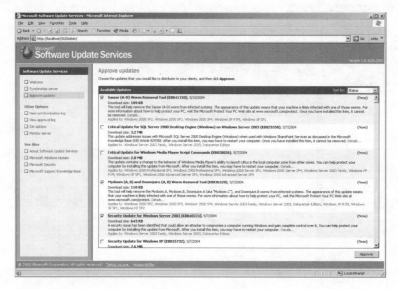

9. In the VBScript message box, click OK to indicate you want to continue approving a new list of updates.

10. You might be asked to accept licensing agreements, depending on the updates you chose to approve.

11. In the VBScript message box indicating that the updates have been successfully approved and are now available to clients, click OK.

EXERCISE 8-4: CONFIGURING THE AUTOMATIC UPDATES CLIENT THROUGH GROUP POLICY

Estimated completion time: 15 minutes

Before installing updates on domain controllers, you test them on an isolated test network to be sure that they do not adversely affect critical applications. Once the testing is complete, you want the domain controllers to receive the updates from a local SUS server automatically. Installation of new updates should occur at 5 A.M. every day, when the SUS servers and the network are unlikely to be very busy.

The following steps will create a new Group Policy Object (GPO) attached to the Domain Controllers organizational unit (OU), which will enforce custom SUS client settings.

> **NOTE** Complete the following exercise on both even-numbered computers.

1. From the Start menu, point to Administrative Tools, and then select Group Policy Management.

2. In the Group Policy Management Console, in the scope pane, expand Forest: Contosoyy.local, expand Domains, expand Contosoyy.local, select and then right-click the Domain Controllers OU, and then select Create And Link A GPO Here.

3. In the New GPO dialog box, in the Name text box, type **Software Updates**, and then click OK.

4. In the Group Policy Management Console, in the scope pane, right-click Software Updates, and select Edit.

5. In the Group Policy Object Editor, under Computer Configuration, expand Administrative Templates, expand Windows Components, and then select Windows Update, as shown in the following example.

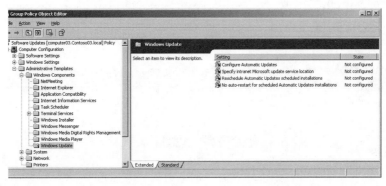

6. In the details pane, double-click Configure Automatic Updates.

7. In the Configure Automatic Updates Properties dialog box, in the Setting tab, select Enabled.

8. In the Configure Automatic Updating drop-down list, select Auto Download And Schedule The Install.

9. In the Schedule Install Day drop-down list, ensure that 0—Every Day is selected. In the Schedule Install Time drop-down list, select 05:00. Click Next Setting.

10. In the Specify Intranet Microsoft Update Service Location Properties dialog box, select Enabled.

11. In the Set The Intranet Update Service For Detecting Updates and the Set The Intranet Statistics Server text boxes, type **http://Computer*zz*,** as shown in the following example from Computer04. Click Next Setting twice.

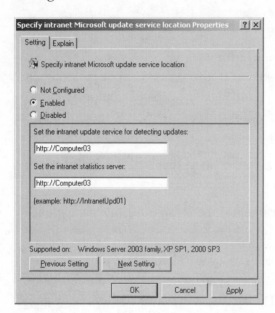

12. In the No Auto-Restart For Scheduled Automatic Updates Installations dialog box, select Enabled.

> **QUESTION**   If you selected Disabled instead, how would the behavior change from the default (Not Configured)? Hint: Click the Explain tab to learn more about what this setting actually does.

13. Click OK. Close the Group Policy Object Editor.

14. From the Start menu, select Run.

15. In the Run dialog box, in the Open text box, type **cmd**, and press ENTER.

16. At the command prompt, type **gpupdate**, and press ENTER.

17. Type **regedit**, and press ENTER.

18. In the Registry Editor, under My Computer, expand HKEY_LOCAL _MACHINE, expand Software, expand Policies, expand Microsoft, expand Windows, and select WindowsUpdate.

QUESTION   What are the values for the WUServer and WUStatusServer keys?

TIP   Steps 17 and 18 have you confirm that the GPO has been applied by viewing the registry. However, checking the Automatic Updates tab in the System Properties dialog box can also serve as a check to see if policies have been applied as intended.

19. Close the Registry Editor and the command prompt window. Leave the Group Policy Management Console open for the Lab Cleanup section.

EXERCISE 8-5: MONITORING SOFTWARE UPDATE SERVICES

Estimated completion time: 5 minutes

To understand which updates are available, to know whether they have been synchronized successfully, and to determine which have been approved, you must browse the various logs associated with SUS.

IMPORTANT   Complete the following exercise on both odd-numbered computers.

1. On the Software Update Services Web site (*http://localhost/SUSAdmin*), in the navigation pane, select View Synchronization Log.

QUESTION   Judging from the contents, what type of information is recorded in the Synchronization Log?

2. In the navigation pane, click View Approval Log.

QUESTION   How many updates are shown as approved in the Approval Log?

3. In the navigation pane, click Monitor Server.

QUESTION   What is shown on the Monitor Server page?

4. From the Start menu, point to Administrative Tools, and select Event Viewer.

5. In the Event Viewer dialog box, in the scope pane, select System.

> **TIP**   In the details pane, search for an event with the source WUSync-Service, and double-click it. An example of the Event Properties is shown in the following figure.
>
> These events will audit whether your SUS server synchronized correctly or whether errors occurred. For example, if Internet connectivity failed during a synchronization attempt, you would see errors and warnings.

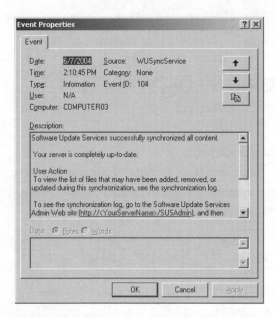

LAB CLEANUP

To complete the lab challenges, you must remove settings for the Automatic Updates clients. This is also important to prevent any updates from being applied, which could affect future labs.

> **IMPORTANT**   Complete the following steps on even-numbered computers.

1. In the Group Policy Management Console (you might already be in the right location), in the scope pane, expand Forest: Contosoyy.local, expand Domains, expand Contosoyy.local, expand Domain Controllers, select and then right-click Software Updates, and select Delete.

2. In the Group Policy Management message box, click OK to confirm that you want to delete the link.

3. Open a command prompt window.

4. From the command prompt, type **gpupdate**, and press ENTER. Close the command prompt window. Close the Group Policy Management Console.

LAB REVIEW QUESTIONS

Estimated completion time: 15 minutes

1. What is the default Uniform Resource Locator (URL) for the SUS Administration Web site?

2. Which component of Windows Server 2003 must first be installed before SUS can be installed?

3. In this lab you created a strict parent/child topology between two SUS servers. How could you change that to a loose parent/child topology? (Hint: Recall the context of the inline question asking about topology in Exercise 8-3.)

4. At Contoso, a SUS parent server has been scheduled to synchronize with the Windows Update servers at 2 A.M. each morning. When you arrive at work at 8 A.M., the Internet connection is working only intermittently, and you want to ensure that the synchronization completed successfully. Which log should you view?

5. You receive an e-mail from Proseware, Inc., a software vendor that created the software application used by the call centers at Contoso; the e-mail indicates that an update released by Microsoft can cause problems with the call center software. Proseware recommends that you do not install the update until Proseware releases a fix for its software. Which log can you view to determine if this update was approved on the parent server?

LAB CHALLENGE 8-1: CONFIGURING WINDOWS UPDATE THROUGH REGISTRY SETTINGS

Estimated completion time: 25 minutes

In a non–Active Directory environment, to change Windows Update settings you must create registry keys and values.

A description of the various registry settings concerning Windows Update can be found in the white paper entitled "SUS Deployment SP1," which can be found in the Lab08 folder in C:\Lab Manual. This white paper is included specifically for use in this lab challenge.

Edit your registry to configure Windows Update according to the following:

- Updates should be automatically downloaded, and installation should occur every day at 2 A.M.

- Automatic Updates should download updates from the SUS server named SUSServer1. This is also the location at which related statistics should be stored.

> **NOTE** This challenge has you configure SUSServer1 as the SUS server for your SUS client. This is purposefully a nonexistent SUS server. The SUS servers configured earlier in this lab are not configured as the SUS server in this challenge to avoid creating any dependencies in future labs that might arise if approved updates were installed.
>
> Also, on the even-numbered computers, some of the registry values you need to create might already exist. In this case, just edit them according to the scenario.

- Automatic Updates should be rescheduled for 10 minutes after startup if the previous scheduled update was missed.

- The computer should not restart on behalf of newly installed updates without permission from the logged-on user.

LAB CHALLENGE 8-2: BACKING UP SOFTWARE UPDATE SERVICES

Estimated completion time: 10 minutes

You have successfully installed SUS and need to back up the metadata. You are unconcerned with backing up the updates because they can simply be downloaded again if necessary.

To complete this lab challenge, create a backup of the metadata in a file called SUSmetadata. The metadata is stored by IIS and contains the configuration information for the SUS server and information about the updates. It does not contain the updates themselves.

> **IMPORTANT** Complete this lab challenge on the odd-numbered computers only.

LAB 9
SECURING NETWORK COMMUNICATION

This lab contains the following exercises and activities:

- Exercise 9-1: Monitoring Unsecured FTP Traffic

- Exercise 9-2: Securing FTP Traffic Using IPSec

- Exercise 9-3: Using the IP Security Monitor Snap-In

- Exercise 9-4: Securing All Data for the FTP Server

- Lab Cleanup

- Lab Review Questions

- Lab Challenge 9-1: Securing Web Traffic with IPSec

SCENARIO

Contoso is creating a File Transfer Protocol (FTP) site to make it easier to exchange data with clients and suppliers. Much of the data that is going to be posted, however, is confidential and will need to be protected.

To protect the credentials used to log on to the FTP site, you are going to create an Internet Protocol Security (IPSec) server that encrypts FTP traffic using filters to target only port 21. You will also configure an IPSec client to create a security association (SA) with the FTP server, which will allow you to decrypt the data. However, encrypting the FTP data over port 21 will not encrypt data that is transferred from the FTP server to FTP clients.

To do this, you will configure an FTP server to secure all Internet Protocol (IP) traffic. This will encrypt both the credentials used to log on to the FTP server and any data transferred between the FTP server and client. IPSec will use Authentication Header (AH) to secure authentication information and will encapsulate data in Encapsulating Security Payload (ESP).

Finally, Contoso is considering using a Web site to provide secure data to clients. However, the Hypertext Transfer Protocol (HTTP) data transmitted over port 80 must be secured (this topic is covered in Lab Challenge 9-1, "Securing Web Traffic with IPSec").

After completing this lab, you will be able to:

- Observe network traffic with Network Monitor
- Create and apply an IPSec policy
- Use the IP Security Monitor snap-in

Estimated completion time: 95 minutes

BEFORE YOU BEGIN

This lab often refers to the number of your domain, your computer, or your partner's computer according to the following conventions:

- *xx* is the number of your domain.
- *yy* is the number of your computer.
- *zz* is the number of your partner's computer.

For example, if you are using Computer04, *xx* = 03 (you are a member of Contoso03.local), *yy* = 04 (you are using Computer04), and *zz* = 03 (your partner is using Computer03).

EXERCISE 9-1: MONITORING UNSECURED FTP TRAFFIC

Estimated completion time: 35 minutes

To secure FTP traffic, you must first install an FTP server. This FTP server is secured later in the lab. You also are going to install the Web publishing service, which will be used in the lab challenge.

To ensure that the data passing through the network is encrypted once you have installed IPSec, you must install Network Monitor so that you can observe network traffic.

Installing Necessary Internet Information Services Components and Network Monitor

The following steps install components of Microsoft Internet Information Services (IIS) and Network Monitor. This is necessary to provide an FTP and Web server and to provide a tool for observing network traffic.

IMPORTANT Ensure that your Microsoft Windows Server 2003 distribution CD is in your CD/DVD drive. If the Welcome To Microsoft Windows Server 2003 screen appears after you insert the CD, close it.

1. Log on with your Administrator account (the password is **P@ssw0rd**).

2. From the Start menu, point to Control Panel, and then select Add Or Remove Programs.

3. In the Add Or Remove Programs window, click the Add/Remove Windows Components icon on the left.

4. In the Windows Components Wizard, on the Windows Components page, in the Components list box, select Management And Monitoring Tools (but do not select the check box next to it), and then click Details.

5. In the Management And Monitoring Tools dialog box, select the Network Monitor Tools check box, and then click OK.

6. In the Windows Components Wizard, on the Windows Components page, select Application Server, and then click Details.

7. In the Application Server dialog box, select the Internet Information Services (IIS) check box if it is not already checked and shaded, and then click Details.

8. In the Internet Information Services dialog box, select the File Transfer Protocol check box, and then click OK.

9. In the Application Server dialog box, click OK.

10. In the Windows Components Wizard dialog box, click Next.

11. The Configuring Components page will appear and indicate progress.

12. On the Completing The Windows Components Wizard page, click Finish.

13. Close the Add Or Remove Programs window.

Configuring File Transfer Protocol

The following steps add a file to the root FTP directory, which is used later to test encryption. Also, you will log on to the FTP server to ensure that it is working.

1. In Windows Explorer or My Computer, browse to C:\Inetpub\Ftproot.

2. From the File menu, point to New, and select Text Document.

3. For the name of the text document, type **Data.txt**, and then press ENTER.

4. Open the Data text document.

5. In the Data.txt file in Notepad, type **THIS IS CONFIDENTIAL INFORMATION**. From the File menu, select Exit.

> **NOTE**   The sentence is in all capitals so that it will be easier to spot when you look for it in network traffic with Network Monitor.

6. In the Notepad message box, click Yes to save changes.

7. From the Start menu, point to Administrative Tools, and then select Internet Information Services (IIS) Manager.

8. In the Internet Information Services (IIS) Manager console, in the scope pane, under Computeryy, select FTP Sites.

9. From the Action menu, select Properties.

10. In the FTP Sites Properties dialog box, in the Security Accounts tab, clear the Allow Anonymous Connections check box.

> **QUESTION**   About what does the IIS Manager message box warn?

11. In the IIS Manager message box, click Yes to indicate that you want to continue.

12. In the FTP Sites Properties dialog box, click OK.

13. Close the Internet Information Services (IIS) Manager console.

14. Open Microsoft Internet Explorer. An Internet Explorer message box might appear and can be dismissed by selecting the Do Not Show This Message Again check box and then clicking OK.

> **IMPORTANT**   Wait until your partner has completed step 14 before continuing.

15. In Internet Explorer, in the Address text box, type **ftp://Computerzz**, and then press ENTER.

16. In the Log On As dialog box, enter your Administrator credentials, as shown in the following example, and then click Log On.

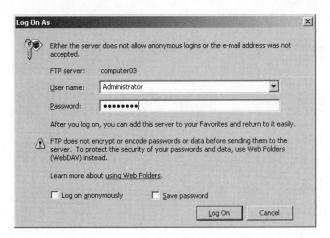

17. After logging on, close Internet Explorer.

Using Network Monitor to View Unsecured FTP Data Transfer

The following steps use Network Monitor to show how easy it is to gather sensitive information on an unprotected network resource. Both the credentials and the data passed by FTP can be easily intercepted and read.

1. From the Start menu, point to Administrative Tools, and then select Network Monitor.

2. In the Microsoft Network Monitor message box, click OK.

3. In the Select A Network dialog box, expand Local Computer, and then select Local Area Connection. The Properties list box should populate with information, as shown in the following example. Click OK.

IMPORTANT   Wait until your partner has completed step 3 before continuing.

4. In Microsoft Network Monitor, click the Start Capture button in the toolbar (or press F10).

5. Launch Internet Explorer, and go to *ftp://Computerzz*.

6. In the Log On As dialog box, enter your Administrator credentials, and then click Log On.

7. In Microsoft Network Monitor, click the Stop And View Capture button (or press SHIFT+F11).

8. Ensure that the Capture: 1 (Summary) window is active, and from the Display menu, select Filter.

9. In the Display Filter dialog box, in the expression tree, select Protocol == Any, and then click Edit Expression.

10. In the Expression dialog box, click Disable All.

11. In the Disabled Protocols list box, select FTP, and then click Enable. FTP is now configured as the only protocol to view. Click OK. FTP should be indicated as the only protocol to allow through the filter, as shown in the following figure.

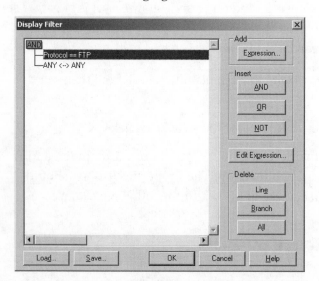

12. In the Display Filter dialog box, click OK.

13. In the Capture: 1 (Summary) window, search for consecutive frames that reveal in the Description column what the user name and password are that were used to access the FTP site on either your computer or your partner's computer. Packets 41 and 42 in the following example fit these criteria.

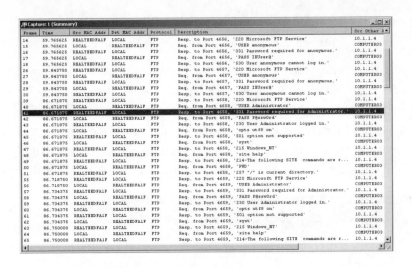

QUESTION   What is the tag that identifies the password?

NOTE   You might notice that before the packets identifying credentials, there are packets indicating a failed attempt at anonymous logon. This is because the FTP client first tried to log on anonymously and was denied. This denial prompts the client to request credentials from the user, which are then passed to the FTP server.

14. Click the Local Area Connection Capture Window (Station Stats) title bar to make that window active.

15. Click the Start Capture button (or press F10).

16. In the Internet Explorer window, copy the Data.txt file to your desktop.

IMPORTANT   If your Internet security settings are too high, you will be denied the capability to complete step 16. You can deal with this in a couple of ways. The best is to add your partner's FTP site (ftp://computeryy) to the list of trusted sites. Alternately, select Options from the Tools menu, and in the Internet Options dialog box, in the Security tab, click Default Level. Adjust the slider to the Medium position, and click OK. This is not recommended in a production environment because security is weakened more broadly than is necessary. Complete step 16.

17. In Microsoft Network Monitor, click the Stop And Capture button (or press SHIFT+F11).

18. Ensure that the Capture: 2 (Summary) window is active, and filter everything but the FTP and Transmission Control Protocol (TCP) frames (use the same technique as in steps 9 through 12 of this exercise).

19. Observe the FTP frames that have the Data.txt file text string in the Description column.

20. Now you need to find the clear text that was inside the Data.txt file you transferred. It will be contained in a TCP packet shortly after an FTP packet that contains within the description the text: `Data connection already open; Transfer startin'`. The frame 98 in the following figure contains the clear text data, whereas the preceding FTP frame contains the telltale message in the description column.

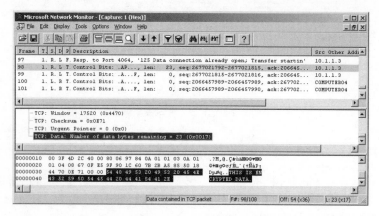

21. Leave Microsoft Network Monitor open for the next exercise. Close Internet Explorer.

EXERCISE 9-2: SECURING FTP TRAFFIC USING IPSEC

Estimated completion time: 35 minutes

As demonstrated in the previous exercise, the information on your FTP server is unsecure. To increase security of credentials passed by FTP, you are going to implement IPSec (which utilizes the AH protocol to handle secure authentication). You should use filters to limit the application of IPSec to only FTP traffic on port 21. In Exercise 9-4, "Securing All Data for the FTP Server," you configure a rule to encrypt all IP traffic so that the data passed will also be secure. For the time being, however, to demonstrate the use of filters, you encrypt only FTP traffic over port 21.

Creating an IPSec Console

The following steps create a Microsoft Management Console (MMC) with the IP Security Monitor and IP Security Policy Management snap-ins. You will use this console to institute IPSec policy on your computer.

1. From the Start menu, select Run.

2. In the Run dialog box, in the Open text box, type **mmc**, and press ENTER.

3. In the Console1 console, from the File menu, select Add/Remove Snap-In.

4. In the Add/Remove Snap-In dialog box, in the Standalone tab, click Add.

5. In the Add Standalone Snap-In dialog box, in the Available Standalone Snap-Ins list box, select IP Security Monitor, and click Add.

6. Select IP Security Policy Management, and then click Add.

7. In the Select Computer Or Domain dialog box, ensure that Local Computer is selected, and then click Finish.

8. In the Add Standalone Snap-In dialog box, click Close.

9. In the Add/Remove Snap-In dialog box, click OK.

10. In the Console1 console, from the File menu, select Save.

11. In the Save As dialog box, save the MMC as **IPSec Policy** on your desktop (the default location is the Administrative Tools folder, but you should save it on your desktop instead for convenient access during this lab).

Configuring an IPSec Policy to Encrypt FTP Traffic

The following steps create an IPSec policy to secure the FTP traffic from and to your FTP server. Your credentials, which are passed on port 21 in FTP, will be encrypted. However, the data, which is passed in TCP over port 20, will not be.

IMPORTANT *Complete the following task on the even-numbered computer.*

1. In the IPSec Policy console, in the scope pane, select and then right-click IP Security Policies On Local Computer, and then select Create IP Security Policy.

2. In the IP Security Policy Wizard, on the Welcome To The IP Security Policy Wizard page, click Next.

3. On the IP Security Policy Name page, in the Name text box, type **FTP Encryption**, and then click Next.

4. On the Request For Secure Communication page, clear the Activate The Default Response Rule check box, and then click Next.

5. On the Completing The IP Security Policy Wizard page, click Finish.

6. In the FTP Encryption Properties dialog box, in the Rules tab, ensure that the Use Add Wizard check box is selected, and then click Add.

7. In the Security Rule Wizard dialog box, on the Welcome To The Create IP Security Rule Wizard page, click Next.

8. On the Tunnel Endpoint page, ensure that This Rule Does Not Specify A Tunnel is selected, and then click Next.

9. On the Network Type page, verify that All Network Connections is selected, and then click Next.

10. On the IP Filter List page, click Add.

11. In the IP Filter List dialog box, in the Name text box, type **FTP**, and click Add.

12. In the IP Filter Wizard, on the Welcome To The IP Filter Wizard page, click Next.

13. On the IP Filter Description And Mirrored Property page, in the Description text box, type **FTP Filter, Port 21 only**. Ensure that the Mirrored check box is selected. Click Next.

14. On the IP Traffic Source page, in the Source Address drop-down list, select Any IP Address, and then click Next.

15. On the IP Traffic Destination page, in the Destination Address list box, select My IP Address, and then click Next.

16. On the IP Protocol Type page, in the Select A Protocol Type drop-down list, select TCP, and then click Next.

17. On the IP Protocol Port page, select To This Port, and in the associated text box, type **21**. Click Next.

18. On the Completing The IP Filter Wizard page, click Finish.

19. In the IP Filter List page, click OK.

20. In the Security Rule Wizard, on the IP Filter List page, in the IP Filter Lists list box, select FTP. Click Next.

21. On the Filter Action page, select Require Security, and then click Next.

22. On the Authentication Method page, verify that Active Directory Default (Kerberos V5 Protocol) is selected, and then click Next.

23. On the Completing The Security Rule Wizard page, click Finish.

24. In the New Rule Properties dialog box, click OK.

25. In the FTP Encryption Properties dialog box, click OK.

26. In the IPSec Policy console, in the details pane, right-click FTP Encryption, and then select Assign.

27. Open the Run dialog box. In the Open text box, type **cmd**, and then press ENTER.

28. At the command prompt, type **net stop policyagent**, and then press ENTER.

29. At the command prompt, type **net start policyagent**, and then press ENTER.

> **NOTE**   By stopping and starting IPSec-related services, you ensure that the new policy will be activated.

30. Close the command prompt window.

> **IMPORTANT**   Complete the following steps on the odd-numbered computer.

31. In the IPSec Policy console, in the scope pane, select IP Security Policies On Local Computer.

32. In the details pane, right-click Client (Respond Only), and then select Assign.

> **IMPORTANT**   Complete the following steps on the even-numbered computer.

33. In Microsoft Network Monitor, click the Local Area Connection Capture Window (Station Stats) title bar to make that window active.

34. Click the Start Capture button (or press F10).

> **IMPORTANT**   Complete the following steps on the odd-numbered computer.

35. Launch Internet Explorer, and log on with your Administrator credentials to *ftp://Computerzz*.

36. Copy the Data file to your desktop. In the Confirm File Replace message box, click Yes to replace the file.

> **IMPORTANT**   Complete the following steps on the even-numbered computer.

37. In Microsoft Network Monitor, click the Stop And View Capture button (or press SHIFT+F11).

38. Ensure that the Capture: 3 (Summary) window is active, and filter everything but the FTP frames (use the same technique as described in Exercise 9-1, "Monitoring Unsecured FTP Traffic," steps 9 through 12 in the "Using Network Monitor to View Unsecured FTP Data Transfer" section).

39. In the Microsoft Network Monitor message box, click OK.

> **QUESTION**   Why are there no FTP frames to display?

40. Filter out all frames except ESP frames.

> **QUESTION**   Is it possible to learn the credentials anymore by reading the Description column? Why or why not?

EXERCISE 9-3: USING THE IP SECURITY MONITOR SNAP-IN

Estimated completion time: 5 minutes

To become familiar with the IP Security Monitor snap-in, which can be useful for troubleshooting, you can examine the IP security settings on your computer using the snap-in. The IP Security Monitor snap-in can be useful for determining which policies are configured and which traffic is being secured.

1. In the IPSec Policy console, in the scope pane, expand IP Security Monitor, and then select Active Policy.

> **QUESTION**   Which policies are currently active?

2. In the scope pane, select Main Mode, and explore the contents in the details pane.

> **QUESTION**   What SAs have been formed with whom, and what type of encryption do they use?

> **QUESTION**   On the even-numbered computer, in the Specific Filters node, why is the FTP Filter, Port 21 Only listed twice?

EXERCISE 9-4: SECURING ALL DATA FOR THE FTP SERVER

Estimated completion time: 10 minutes

Now that you have successfully encrypted just the FTP data transmitted over port 21, you decide that the clear text data needs to be encrypted as well. Therefore, you are going to change the IPSec policy on the FTP server to be Secure Server

(Require Security). This will ensure that all IP traffic to and from the server is secure. AH will handle authentication, and data will be secured in ESP. Once you have secured the traffic, you will use Network Monitor to confirm the encryption.

> **IMPORTANT**   *Complete the following steps on the even-numbered computer.*

1. In the IPSec Policy console, in the scope pane, select IP Security Policies On Local Computer.

2. In the Details pane, right-click Secure Server (Require Security), and then select Assign.

3. Stop and start the policyagent (use the command lines **net stop policyagent** and **net start policyagent**).

4. In Microsoft Network Monitor, click the Local Area Connection Capture Window (Station Stats) title bar to make that window active.

5. Click the Start Capture button (or press F10).

> **IMPORTANT**   *Complete the following steps from the odd-numbered computer.*

6. Launch Internet Explorer, and log on with your Administrator credentials to *ftp://Computerzz*.

7. Copy the Data.txt file to your desktop. In the Confirm File Replace message box, click Yes to replace the file.

> **IMPORTANT**   *Complete the following steps from the even-numbered computer.*

8. In Microsoft Network Monitor, click the Stop And View Capture button (or press SHIFT+F11).

9. Ensure that the Capture: 3 (Summary) window is active. Note that all the frames are in the ESP protocol.

> **QUESTION**   *Why are the frames all in ESP?*

> **QUESTION**   *Can you find either the credential information or the clear text within the Data.txt file in any of the packets?*

10. Close Microsoft Network Monitor, and don't save any data when prompted.

LAB CLEANUP

Estimated completion time: 5 minutes
The following steps restore the original IPSec policies. If the lab challenge is completed, this should be completed after it as well to ensure that future labs are not harmed by dependencies.

1. In the IPSec Policy console, in the scope pane, select IP Security Policies On Local Computer.

2. From the Action menu, point to All Tasks, and then select Restore Default Policies.

3. In the IP Security Policy Management message box, click Yes to indicate that you want to continue.

4. Click OK in the IP Security Policy Management message box confirming that default policies were restored to initial settings.

5. On the odd-numbered computer, in the details pane, select Client (Respond Only), and from the Action menu, select Un-Assign.

6. On the even-numbered computer, in the details pane, select Secure Server (Require Security), and from the Action menu, select Un-Assign.

LAB REVIEW QUESTIONS

Estimated completion time: 15 minutes

1. Which snap-ins are used in relation to IPSec on a server running Microsoft Server 2003?

2. When IPSec is used to encrypt the data of a particular protocol, such as FTP, what type of frames encapsulate the original frames (which are encrypted)?

3. Which command-line command string will stop the IPSec service, and which will start it again?

4. Imagine that in a situation such as that created in the lab, a hacker is able to determine which ESP frames in a transmission are responsible for supplying credential information to an FTP server (user name and password) and capture them. Even though the frames are encrypted, the data within is still valid. The hacker then sends this information from his own computer to try to use it to log on to the FTP server. What type of security measure is responsible for thwarting this type of attack?

LAB CHALLENGE 9-1: SECURING WEB TRAFFIC WITH IPSEC

Estimated completion time: 40 minutes

Contoso has recently set up a Web site that allows vendors to check invoices and invoice histories. Currently, the Web site has not been deployed because the information on it is not secure.

As part of the security measures, you have been asked to configure IPSec on the Web site. To complete this lab challenge, do the following with your partner:

- Copy the Default.htm file from C:\Lab Manual\Lab09 to C:\Inetpub \wwwroot\ on the odd-numbered computer.

- Create an IPSec policy on the odd-numbered computer that encrypts traffic for HTTP over port 80. Set the policy to accept secure traffic only.

- Make the even-numbered computer an IPSec client.

- Using Network Monitor, confirm that the HTTP frames have been encapsulated in ESP frames.

LAB 10
SECURITY CERTIFICATE AUTHORITIES

This lab contains the following exercises and activities:

- Exercise 10-1: Installing an Enterprise Root Certificate Authority

- Exercise 10-2: Installing a Subordinate Enterprise Certificate Authority

- Exercise 10-3: Receiving a Certificate Through the Encrypting File System

- Exercise 10-4: Creating and Publishing a Custom, Version 2 Certificate Template

- Exercise 10-5: Requesting a Certificate Through Web Enrollment

- Exercise 10-6: Revoking a Certificate

- Lab Cleanup

- Lab Review Questions

- Lab Challenge 10-1: Configuring and Testing Stand-Alone Root and Subordinate Certificate Authorities

SCENARIO

Currently, the Contoso network relies on outside certification authorities or internal, low-trust authorities for certificates for encryption and authentication. For example, when a user encrypts a file, Encrypting File System (EFS) relies on the local computer to issue a certificate to the user, but the certificate is not a trusted certificate, because it is not from a trusted source. Furthermore, Contoso is planning on using smart cards for authentication for high-security accounts, and you need to be able to publish a custom smart card logon that enables all domain users to enroll for the certificate.

To deal with these issues, you must create a CA hierarchy of a root and subordinate CA, which will handle all certificates that are issued for internal purposes.

After completing this lab, you will be able to:

- Install and configure enterprise and stand-alone certificate authorities (CAs)
- Request certificates and view them with the Certificates snap-in
- Create and publish version 2 certificates
- Use Web enrollment for obtaining certificates
- Revoke certificates

Estimated completion time: 120 minutes

BEFORE YOU BEGIN

If you did not do so in the Before You Begin section of Lab 5, "Software Deployment and Restrictions Using Group Policy," Lab 6, "Microsoft Windows Server 2003 Security Configuration," or Lab 7, "Security Templates," you must run the ADUCUpdatexx.vbs file located in C:\Lab Manual\Lab05. This script creates the structure pictured in Figure 10-1.

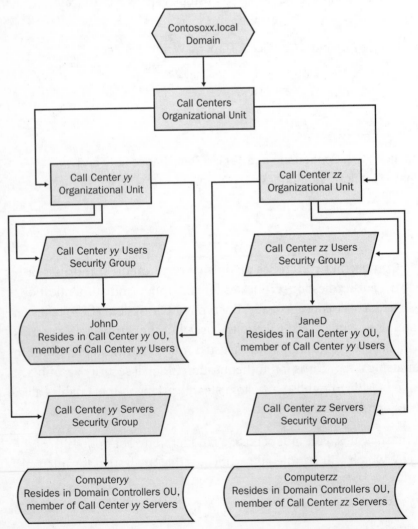

Figure 10-1 The ADUCUpdate*xx*.vbs script creates this structure within Active Directory

Also, a software restriction on Notepad was implemented in Lab 5, Exercise 5-5, "Restricting Software Through Group Policy Using Paths," and Exercise 5-6, "Restricting Software Through Group Policy Using a Hash." These restrictions must be deleted if they haven't been already. To delete these restrictions, simply follow the corresponding exercises in Lab 5 to locate the restriction, select it, press DELETE, and then confirm the deletion.

This lab often refers to the number of your domain, your computer, or your partner's computer according to the following conventions:

- *xx* is the number of your domain.

- *yy* is the number of your computer.

- *zz* is the number of your partner's computer.

For example, if you are using Computer04, $xx = 03$ (you are a member of Contoso03.local), $yy = 04$ (you are using Computer04), and $zz = 03$ (your partner is using Computer03).

EXERCISE 10-1: INSTALLING AN ENTERPRISE ROOT CERTIFICATE AUTHORITY

Estimated completion time: 20 minutes

The first step in implementing the CA hierarchy is to establish a root CA. Because compromising the root CA is potentially very harmful, the certificate should employ a 4-kilobyte (KB) key length, which is longer than the default and therefore more secure.

The following exercise configures your server to run Certificate Services as an enterprise root CA.

> **IMPORTANT** Complete the following exercise on the odd-numbered computer.

> **NOTE** Ensure that your Microsoft Windows Server 2003 distribution CD is in your CD/DVD drive. If the Welcome To Microsoft Windows Server 2003 page opens after you insert the CD, close it.

1. Log on with your Administrator account (the password is **P@ssw0rd**).

2. From the Start menu, point to Control Panel, and then select Add Or Remove Programs.

3. In the Add Or Remove Programs window, click the Add/Remove Windows Components icon on the left.

4. In the Windows Components Wizard, on the Windows Components page, select Application Server (but do not select the check box next to it), and then click Details.

5. In the Application Server dialog box, select the ASP.NET check box (if the Internet Information Services (IIS) check box is not selected and shaded, select it also). Click OK.

> **NOTE** This lab uses the World Wide Web service, also. Ensure that World Wide Web Service within Internet Information Services (IIS) is selected.

6. In the Windows Components Wizard, on the Windows Components page, click Next.

7. On the Completing The Windows Components Wizard page, click Finish.

8. In the Add Or Remove Programs window, click the Add/Remove Windows Components icon on the left.

9. In the Windows Components Wizard, on the Windows Components page, select Certificate Services, and then click Next.

10. In the Microsoft Certificate Services message box, click Yes.

> **QUESTION** What is the warning conveyed in the Microsoft Certificate Services message box?

11. On the CA Type page, ensure that Enterprise Root CA is selected, select the Use Custom Settings To Generate The Key Pair And CA Certificates check box, and then click Next.

12. On the Public And Private Key Pair page, in the Key Length drop-down list, select 4096. Leave the other selections with their default settings, and then click Next.

> **QUESTION** Which computer resource is taxed most by using longer key lengths?

13. On the CA Identifying Information page, in the Common Name For This CA text box, type **Contoso*xx* CA Root**. An example from Computer03 is shown in the following figure. Click Next.

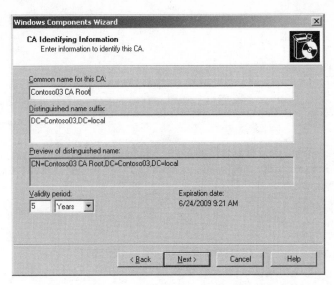

14. The Cryptographic Key Generation page will appear briefly.

> **QUESTION**   Why are cryptographic keys being created during the installation of a root CA?

15. On the Certificate Database Settings page, accept the default locations of the database and database log, and then click Next.

16. In the Microsoft Certificate Services message box, click Yes to confirm that it is okay to halt IIS temporarily.

17. The Configuring Components page will indicate installation progress. Installation will be interrupted by a Microsoft Certificate Services message box asking if you want to enable Active Server Pages (ASP). Click Yes.

> **NOTE**   Depending on the order in which Certificate Services, IIS, and ASP are installed, steps 16 and 17 might not be necessary.

> **QUESTION**   For what purpose is ASP used by Certificate Services?

18. On the Completing The Windows Components Wizard page, click Finish.

19. Close the Add Or Remove Programs window.

EXERCISE 10-2: INSTALLING A SUBORDINATE ENTERPRISE CERTIFICATE AUTHORITY

Estimated completion time: 10 minutes

Now that the root CA is established, a subordinate CA can be installed, which will handle the normal certificate requests (requests for renewals of certificates for subordinate CAs, and for the root CA itself, will have to be handled by the root

CA). Because the subordinate CA is not as valuable a target as the root CA, the encryption key need be only 1 KB.

> **IMPORTANT**   *Complete the following exercise on the even-numbered computer. Do not begin these steps until Exercise 10-1, "Installing an Enterprise Root Certificate Authority," has been completed.*

> **NOTE**   *Ensure that your Windows Server 2003 distribution CD is in your CD/DVD drive. If the Welcome To Microsoft Windows Server 2003 page opens after you insert the CD, close it.*

1. Complete steps 1 through 10 of Exercise 10-1.

2. On the CA Type page, ensure that Enterprise Subordinate CA is selected, and then click Next.

3. On the CA Identifying Information page, in the Common Name For This CA text box, type **Contoso*xx* CA Subordinate**, and then click Next.

4. On the Certificate Database Settings page, click Next to accept the default location for the database and database log.

5. On the CA Certificate Request page, ensure that the Send The Request To A CA Already On The Network is selected.

6. In the Computer Name text box, type **Computer*zz***.

7. Click the Parent CA list box (the Computer Name text box should populate with the fully qualified domain name (FQDN) of your partner's computer), and ensure that Contoso03 CA Root is selected. An example from Computer03 is shown in the following figure. Click Next.

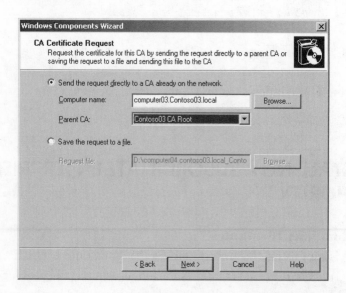

QUESTION Why is the installation of the subordinate CA requesting a certificate from the root CA?

8. In the Microsoft Certificate Services message box, click Yes to confirm that it is okay to temporarily halt IIS.

9. The Configuring Components page will indicate installation progress. Installation will be interrupted by a Microsoft Certificate Services message box asking if you want to enable ASP. Click Yes.

NOTE Depending on the order in which Certificate Services, IIS, and ASP are installed, steps 8 and 9 might not be necessary.

10. On the Completing The Windows Components Wizard page, click Finish.

11. Close the Add Or Remove Programs window.

EXERCISE 10-3: RECEIVING A CERTIFICATE THROUGH THE ENCRYPTING FILE SYSTEM

Estimated completion time: 40 minutes

Now that you have set up a root CA and a subordinate CA in your domain, you want to make sure they are working properly. After checking each CA, you should set the root CA offline (stop the service) for security reasons.

NOTE For security reasons, it is a best practice to remove an important root CA from the network entirely, except when it needs to issue or renew certificates (this can also be done by file transfer, so that the root CA can always be off the network). However, for the internal purposes of an enterprise, it might be enough to turn off the service on the enterprise root CA and allow the subordinate CAs to do the work. This is especially true if the CA is used only for internal security, and outside organizations are not required to trust the CA.

To test the CAs, you have decided to have a domain user request a certificate by using EFS.

MORE INFO EFS requires a certificate because it relies on a public encrypting key and a private decrypting key.

To see which certificates are issued at the request of EFS and from where they come, you will use the Certificates snap-in.

Requesting a Certificate from the Root Certificate Authority

The following steps use EFS, which requests a certificate.

> **IMPORTANT**   *Complete the following steps on both computers.*

1. Log off and log on as JohnD if your computer number is odd, and JaneD if your computer number is even.

2. Right-click the desktop, point to New, and select Folder. Name the folder **Test1**.

3. Open Test1. In the Test1 folder, from the File menu, point to New, and select Text Document. Accept New Text Document as the name.

4. Open New Text Document.

5. In Notepad, type **Encrypted text**. From the File menu, select Exit, and save changes when prompted.

6. Close the Test1 folder, right-click it, and then select Properties.

7. In the Test1 Properties dialog box, in the General tab, click Advanced.

8. In the Advanced Attributes dialog box, select the Encrypt Contents To Secure Data check box. Click OK.

9. In the Test1 Properties dialog box, click OK.

10. In the Confirm Attribute Changes message box, click OK to apply the changes to the folder, subfolders, and files.

11. Verify that you can read New Text Document in the Test1 folder.

Examining the Certificate

Now that a certificate has been issued at the request of EFS, you want to make sure that it is from an acceptable location and has sufficient trust. To do this, you must first create a console containing the Certificates snap-in.

1. From the Start menu, select Run.

2. In the Run dialog box, in the Open text box, type **mmc**, and press ENTER.

3. In the Console1 console, from the File menu, select Add/Remove Snap-In.

4. In the Add/Remove Snap-In dialog box, in the Stand-Alone tab, click Add.

5. In the Add Stand-Alone Snap-In dialog box, select Certificates, and click Add. Click Close.

6. In the Add/Remove Snap-In dialog box, click OK.

7. In the Console1 console, from the File menu, select Save. Save the console on the desktop as Certificates Manager.

8. In the Certificates Manager console, in the scope pane, expand Certificates, expand Personal, and then select Certificates. In the Details pane, double-click JohnD or JaneD.

9. Examine the Certificate dialog box (all the tabs), and answer the following questions:

> **QUESTION** What is the purpose of the certificate?

> **QUESTION** From which CA was the certificate issued?

> **QUESTION** How far apart are the Valid From and Valid To dates for the certificate?

> **QUESTION** What is the certification path, from leaves to root?

10. In the Certificate dialog box, click OK. Leave the Certificate Manager console open.

Receiving a Certificate from a Subordinate Certificate Authority

> **IMPORTANT** Complete steps 1 through 3 on the odd-numbered computer only.

1. In Windows Explorer, or through My Computer, browse to C:\Windows\System32, right-click Certsrv.msc, and then select Run As. (You might find it easier to find Certsrv.msc by using Search.)

2. In the Run As dialog box, select The Following User, enter your Administrator credentials, and then click OK.

3. In the Certification Authority console, in the scope pane, select Contoso*xx* CA Root. In the toolbar, click the Stop button (it is a black square). This will stop the Certificate Services on the root CA. Close the Certification Authority console.

> **IMPORTANT**   *Complete the following steps on both computers.*

4. Open the Test1 folder, and attempt to open New Text Document. You should be able to.

5. In the Certificates Manager console, in the scope pane, expand Certificates, expand Personal, and then select Certificates.

6. In the details pane, select the EFS certificate (the certificate is named after the user, and the purpose of the certificate is for Encrypting File System), and then press DELETE. In the Certificates message box, click Yes to delete the certificate.

7. Log off and log back on as JohnD or JaneD, as appropriate (don't save changes to the Certificate Manager console).

8. Attempt to open New Text Document in the Test1 folder.

9. In the Notepad message box acknowledging that access is denied, click OK. Close all open windows.

10. Create a folder on the desktop named **Test2**. In the folder, create a text document with the name **New Text Document** that contains the text **Encrypted File**. Encrypt the Test2 folder and all of its contents. This procedure is outlined in steps 2 through 11 of Exercise 10-3, "Receiving a Certificate Through the Encrypting File System."

11. Open the Certificates Manager console, and double-click the certificate that was just created by EFS (it will be under the Personal node in the console tree).

> **QUESTION**   What is the certification path for the certificate, and how does it indicate that the certificate should be trusted?

> **QUESTION**   Will the new certificate allow you to decrypt the Notepad document in the Test1 folder?

EXERCISE 10-4: CREATING AND PUBLISHING A CUSTOM, VERSION 2 CERTIFICATE TEMPLATE

Estimated completion time: 15 minutes

You have been asked to create a custom certificate template that is identical to the Smartcard Logon certificate, except that it needs to enable Domain Users to request the certificate through Web enrollment.

> **NOTE**   For the purposes of the lab, the root CA service will be brought back online. This is not recommended in a real environment, where security is benefited when the root CA is not accessible. However, in a real environment it must be accessible in some way when it is needed to renew essential certificates for maintaining the CA hierarchy. This can be done by bringing it back online, or by using files and removable media to transfer the certificate transactions manually, for extra security.

> **IMPORTANT**   Complete the following steps on both computers.

1. Log on with your Administrator account.

2. Open the Certification Authority console.

> **IMPORTANT**   Complete steps 3 through 10 on the odd-numbered computer only.

3. In the Certification Authority console, start Certificate Services by clicking the Play icon in the toolbar (it is a rightward-pointing black triangle).

4. In the scope pane, expand Contoso*xx* CA Root, select and then right-click Certificate Templates, and then select Manage.

5. In the Certificate Templates console, in the details pane, right-click SmartCard User, and then select Duplicate Template.

6. In the Properties Of New Template dialog box, in the General tab, in the Template Display Name text box, type **Custom Smartcard Logon**.

7. In the Security tab, click Add.

8. In the Select Users, Computers, Or Groups console, in the Enter The Object Names To Select (Examples) text box, type **Domain U**, and then click Check Names. Domain Users should appear. Click OK.

9. In the Properties Of New Template dialog box, select the Allow check box for the Enroll permission, for the Domain Users security group, as shown in the following figure. Click OK.

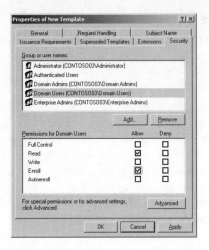

> **QUESTION**   Why is the icon from the Custom Smartcard User certificate template gold, whereas the icon for the Smartcard User certificate template is gray?

10. Close the Certificate Templates console.

> **IMPORTANT**   Complete the following steps on both computers. The Contosoxx CA Subordinate node of the even-numbered computer might need to be expanded before step 11 can be completed.

11. In the Certification Authority console, right-click Certificate Templates, point to New, and then select Certificate Template To Issue.

> **IMPORTANT**   To issue a version 2 certificate template, you must be running Windows Server 2003, Enterprise Edition, or Windows Server 2003, Datacenter Edition.

12. In the Enable Certificate Templates dialog box, select Custom Smartcard User, and then click OK. The Custom Smartcard User certificate template should be added to the Certificate Templates details pane in the Certification Authority console, as shown in the following figure.

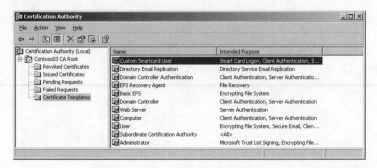

EXERCISE 10-5: REQUESTING A CERTIFICATE THROUGH WEB ENROLLMENT

Estimated completion time: 10 minutes

Now that the Custom Smartcard Logon certificate template has been issued, you want to make sure that ordinary users (domain users) can successfully request and receive it through Web enrollment.

> **IMPORTANT** Complete the following steps on both computers. You might receive security warnings during this exercise issued by Microsoft Internet Explorer. Add your partner's Web site to your list of trusted sites, and choose not to display future warnings when asked.

1. Log on as JohnD or JaneD as appropriate (JohnD on the even-numbered computer and JaneD on the odd-numbered computer).

2. From the Start menu, select Internet Explorer.

3. In Internet Explorer, in the Address text box, type **http://computerzz/certsrv**.

4. In the Connect To Computerzz.Contosoxx.Local dialog box, enter the credentials for JohnD or JaneD, as appropriate.

5. On the Microsoft Certificate Services Web site, under Select A Task, click Request A Certificate.

6. On the Request A Certificate page, click Advanced Certificate Request.

7. On the Advanced Certificate Request page, select Create And Submit A Request To This CA.

8. In the Certificate Template drop-down list, ensure that Custom Smartcard Logon is selected, and then click Submit at the bottom of the page.

9. In the Potential Scripting Violation message box, click Yes to confirm that you want to request the certificate.

> **TIP** If you receive a Failed To Create 'CertificateAuthority.Request' Object error message, the Enable Session State check box might not be selected in the Application Configuration Properties dialog box of the site where the Certificate Server service is running (Windows Server 2003 Certificate Server service uses session states to pass the request for the certificate to the processing page).
>
> To remedy this, open the Internet Information Services (IIS) console, and access the Properties dialog box of the Certsrv Web application (Local Computer|Web Sites|Default Web Site|CertSrv). In the Virtual Directory tab of the CertSrv Properties dialog box, click Configuration. In the Application Configuration dialog box, in the Options tab, select the Enable Session State check box.
>
> After you have made this configuration change, you must restart the IIS Admin Service. This can be done by right-clicking the service in the Services console and selecting Restart.

10. On the Certificate Issued page, click Install This Certificate.

11. In the Potential Scripting Violation message box, click Yes.

12. The Certificate Installed page will appear. Close Internet Explorer.

EXERCISE 10-6: REVOKING A CERTIFICATE

Estimated completion time: 10 minutes

Each time a user leaves the company, you are asked to revoke any certificates that could be a security risk. The following exercise uses the Certification Authority console to revoke a certificate.

1. Log on with your Administrator account.

2. In the Certification Authority console, in the scope pane, expand Contosoxx CA Root on the odd-numbered computer, and Contosoxx CA Subordinate on the even-numbered computer, and then select Issued Certificates.

3. In the details pane, right-click the certificate just requested by your partner (it should be the most recently issued certificate), point to All Tasks, and then select Revoke Certificate.

4. In the Certificate Revocation dialog box, ensure that Unspecified is selected in the Reason Code message box, and then click Yes.

> **QUESTION**   Is there any way to reverse the revocation of a certificate once it is revoked?

5. In the Certification Authority console, select and then right-click Revoked Certificates, point to All Tasks, and then select Publish.

6. In the Publish CRL dialog box, ensure that New CRL is selected, and then click OK.

7. In the Certification Authority console, in the scope pane, select and then right-click Revoked Certificates, and then select Properties.

8. In the Revoked Certificates Properties dialog box, in the View CRLs tab, click View CRL.

9. In the Certificate Revocation List dialog box, in the Revocation List tab, observe that the serial number of the certificate you revoked is in the list, as shown in the following figure.

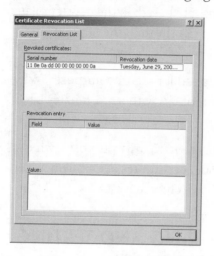

LAB CLEANUP

Estimated completion time: 10 minutes

To complete Lab Challenge 10-1, you must remove Certificate Services.

1. From the Start menu, point to Control Panel, and select Add Or Remove Programs.

2. In the Add Or Remove Programs window, click the Add/Remove Windows Components icon on the left.

3. In the Windows Components Wizard, on the Windows Components page, clear the Certificate Services check box, and then click Next.

4. The Configuring Components page will appear and indicate progress.

5. When the Completing The Windows Components Wizard page appears, click Finish.

6. Close the Add Or Remove Programs window.

LAB REVIEW QUESTIONS

Estimated completion time: 15 minutes

1. What is a certificate?

2. When you publish revoked certificates from an enterprise CA hosted by Windows Server 2003, to what two locations can the CA publish its CRL?

3. You create a new certificate template and set its security settings to allow enrollment for all authenticated users. You create a test account that is a member of the Domain Users and Authenticated Users groups. When you try to obtain a certificate based on the new template with the new account by accessing the CA through the *http://CAhost /certsrv* Web site, the certificate is not available. Why?

4. In the lab, the root CA service was stopped for security purposes. Why is it recommended for security that a root CA with subordinates be made inaccessible?

5. When a root CA is taken off all networks for security purposes, what is the most secure way to have it renew old certificates and issue new certificates when it needs to maintain the CA hierarchy?

LAB CHALLENGE 10-1: CONFIGURING AND TESTING STAND-ALONE ROOT AND SUBORDINATE CERTIFICATE AUTHORITIES

Estimated completion time: 45 minutes

Contoso has recently acquired Litware, Inc., and sometimes users in the two companies require certificates for secure communication and digital signatures. However, the enterprise CAs store their information in Active Directory, and you want CAs that store their information locally, for greater security. Furthermore, you want to approve each certificate request manually.

Therefore, you must configure and test stand-alone CAs. To complete this lab challenge, do the following:

- Install a stand-alone root CA on the even-numbered computer.

- Configure a shared location on the even-numbered computer in a shared folder at C:\CertificateServices. Give Administrators full access and others read-only access.

- Install a stand-alone issuing (subordinate) CA on the odd-numbered computer.

- Stop Certificate Services on the root CA.

- Request a certificate using Web enrollment for e-mail authentication and encryption (one certificate).

- Issue and install the certificate.

LAB 11
CLUSTERING AND AVAILABILITY

This lab contains the following exercises and activities:

■ Exercise 11-1: Configuring a Two-Node Network Load Balancing Cluster

■ Exercise 11-2: Accessing the Web Site Hosted on the Network Load Balancing Cluster

■ Exercise 11-3: Observing and Troubleshooting Network Load Balancing Clusters

■ Lab Cleanup

■ Lab Review Questions

■ Lab Challenge 11-1: Configuring a Local Quorum Server Cluster

SCENARIO

You are a network administrator for Contoso, Ltd. Currently, Contoso hosts critical applications on single servers. There is no failover for the company's Web page (used for advertising), and if the lone server is overwhelmed by too many hits, the customers suffer the resulting sluggishness. To increase both availability and reliability, you are going to create a Network Load Balancing cluster to serve the Web site.

Once you have configured the Network Load Balancing cluster, you will break it in various ways, and use various tools to diagnose what is wrong. These experiments will help to prepare for troubleshooting potential future issues.

Finally, you are going to install a local quorum server cluster, which runs on a single server. Typical server clusters require a shared storage location, known as a quorum drive, which is not available in most lab environments. The local quorum is a special clustering mode that is available for testing and training. Although the local quorum does not provide fault tolerance, it does enable you to explore the clustering software interface.

IMPORTANT You might receive security warnings during this lab issued by Microsoft Internet Explorer. Add any Web sites used to your list of trusted sites, and choose not to display future warnings when asked.

After completing this lab, you will be able to:

- Configure a Network Load Balancing cluster using unicast mode on a multihomed computer to increase availability
- Use Event Viewer, the Network Load Balancing Manager console, and the Nlb command to troubleshoot Network Load Balancing
- Understand the relationship between virtual Internet Protocol (IP) addresses and Media Access Control (MAC) addresses
- Configure a server cluster

Estimated completion time: 95 minutes

BEFORE YOU BEGIN

To complete this lab, you must ensure that the following dependencies are completed.

- This lab requires that a Web server be installed. This is done by selectively installing components of Microsoft Internet Information Services (IIS). The procedure for doing this is in Lab 9, "Securing Network Information with IPSec," Exercise 9-1, "Monitoring Unsecured FTP Traffic." You do not need to install the File Transfer Protocol (FTP) component, only the Web component.
- If it is not already there, copy the Default.htm file from C:\Lab Manual\Lab09 to C:\Inetpub\Wwwroot (this was completed in Lab Challenge 9-1, "Securing Web Traffic with IPSec").

This lab often refers to the number of your domain, your computer, or your partner's computer according to the following conventions:

- *xx* is the number of your domain.
- *yy* is the number of your computer.
- *zz* is the number of your partner's computer.

For example, if you are using Computer04, *xx* = 03 (you are a member of Contoso03.local), *yy* = 04 (you are using Computer04), and *zz* = 03 (your partner is using Computer03).

EXERCISE 11-1: CONFIGURING A TWO-NODE NETWORK LOAD BALANCING CLUSTER

Estimated completion time: 25 minutes

Currently, Contoso hosts its Web site on a single IIS Web server. A combination of more customers visiting the site and making large Portable Document Format (PDF) files available describing the company's products has caused the Web site to become sluggish to outside users.

Also, if for some reason the single server cannot respond to requests, for example, because of a faulty network card, the page becomes unavailable.

To increase availability, and to distribute the heavy load to more servers, you must configure a Network Load Balancing cluster. The Network Load Balancing cluster will use two adapters in each computer, one dedicated to cluster traffic and the other to handle normal network traffic. For the purposes of the lab, the adapters dedicated to the clusters will use a crossover cable between them.

Preparing Your Network

To prepare your network for Network Load Balancing clustering, you must configure the Transmission Control Protocol/Internet Protocol (TCP/IP) properties of your cluster network connection and enable them.

1. Log on with your Administrator account (the password is **P@ssw0rd**).

2. Connect your Cluster network interface card (NIC) to your partner's Cluster NIC using a crossover (swap) cable.

3. From the Start menu, point to Control Panel, and select Network Connections.

4. In the Network Connections window, right-click Cluster, and then select Properties.

5. In the Cluster Properties dialog box, select Internet Protocol (TCP/IP), and then click Properties.

6. In the Internet Protocol (TCP/IP) Properties dialog box, select Use The Following IP Address. In the IP Address text box, type **192.168.0.yy**. In the Subnet Mask text box, type **255.255.255.0**.

7. Select Use The Following DNS Server Addresses. In the Preferred DNS Server text box, type **10.1.1.xx**. Click OK.

8. In the Cluster Properties dialog box, in the General tab, click Install.

9. In the Select Network Connection Type page, select Service, and then click Add.

10. In the Select Network Service dialog box, select Network Load Balancing, and then click OK.

11. In the Cluster Properties dialog box, click Close.

12. You can leave the Network Connections window open because it is used again.

> **NOTE** Use the Ping utility to check connectivity to your partner's Cluster NIC when both computers are configured.

Creating a New Cluster

Now that you have configured your host computers with a NIC dedicated to cluster traffic, you can configure Network Load Balancing.

> **IMPORTANT** Complete the following steps on the odd-numbered computer.

1. From the Start menu, point to Administrative Tools, and then select Network Load Balancing Manager.

2. In the Network Load Balancing Manager console, in the scope pane, select and then right-click Network Load Balancing Clusters, and then select New Cluster.

3. In the Cluster Parameters dialog box, in the IP Address text box, type **192.168.0.1xx**. In the Subnet Mask text box, type **255.255.255.0**, and in the Full Internet Name text box, type **www.Contosoxx.com**.

> **QUESTION** What is the Network Address shown in this dialog box:

4. In the Cluster Operation Mode section, ensure that Unicast is selected.

> **NOTE** Depending on which option you choose, Multicast or Unicast, the network adapter assigned to Network Load Balancing is resolved by Address Resolution Protocol (ARP) to either its original MAC address or to a virtual MAC address, respectively. By choosing Multicast, you can use a single network adapter to handle both cluster traffic and normal network traffic. However, Microsoft best practices suggest that you use a multihomed computer with at least one adapter dedicated to each of these functions. This way internal traffic won't interfere with cluster traffic, and vice versa. Furthermore, using a separate network adapter for the cluster provides greater compatibility among network cards and routers.

5. Your configuration should look similar to the following example from Computer03. Click Next.

6. In the Cluster IP Addresses dialog box, click Add.

7. In the Add/Edit IP Address dialog box, in the IP Address text box, type **192.168.1.1xx**. Click in the Subnet Mask text box, and ensure that **255.255.255.0** is entered. Click OK.

8. In the Cluster IP Addresses dialog box, click Next.

9. In the Port Rules dialog box, click Edit.

10. In the Add/Edit Port Rule dialog box, in the Port Range section, in the From and To text boxes, type **80**. Click OK.

11. In the Port Rules dialog box, click Next.

12. In the Connect dialog box, in the Host text box, type **Computeryy**, and then click Connect.

13. In the Interfaces Available For Configuring A New Cluster list box, select Cluster, and then click Next.

14. In the Host Parameters dialog box, click Finish.

15. In about one minute, the Network Load Balancing Manager console should look similar to the following figure from Computer03.

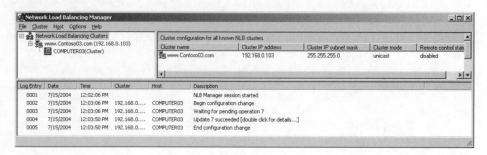

> **IMPORTANT**   *Complete the following steps on the even-numbered computer.*

16. From the Start menu, point to Administrative Tools, and then select Network Load Balancing Manager.

17. In the Network Load Balancing Manager console, in the scope pane, select and then right-click Network Load Balancing Clusters, and then select Connect To Existing.

18. In the Connect dialog box, in the Host text box, type **Computer*zz***, and then click Connect.

19. In the Clusters list box, select www.Contoso*xx*.com, and then click Finish.

20. In the Network Load Balancing Manager console, in the scope pane, select and then right-click www.Contoso*xx*.com (192.168.0.1*xx*), and then select Add Host To Cluster.

21. In the Connect dialog box, in the Host text box, type **Computer*yy***. Click Connect.

22. In the Interfaces Available For Configuring A New Cluster list box, select Cluster, and then click Next.

23. In the Host Parameters dialog box, click Finish.

> **QUESTION**   *When you added the previous host to the new cluster, the Priority number was 1. Why did that number change for the second host?*

24. Once you have added the second computer to the Network Load Balancing cluster, the Network Load Balancing Manager on the even-numbered computer should look similar to the following graphic from Computer04.

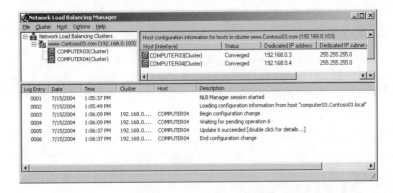

> **TIP** Once you have configured the cluster, you might want to ping the cluster IP addresses to make sure that they respond.

EXERCISE 11-2: ACCESSING THE WEB SITE HOSTED ON THE NETWORK LOAD BALANCING CLUSTER

Estimated completion time: 15 minutes

Now that you have configured the cluster, you note that the Web site no longer can be accessed. After using Nslookup, you determine that this is because the fully qualified domain name (FQDN) of the Web site is resolving to the old address. To fix this, you need to update the Domain Name System (DNS) server with the new IP address for the Web site.

Updating Your DNS Server

The following steps add a new forward lookup zone and a host (A) record to your DNS server for the new IP address of the Web site.

> **IMPORTANT** Complete the following steps on the odd-numbered computer.

1. From the Start menu, point to Administrative Tools, and then select DNS.

2. In the DNS Management console, right-click COMPUTERyy, and then select New Zone.

3. In the New Zone Wizard, on the Welcome To The New Zone Wizard page, click Next.

4. On the Zone Type page, ensure that Primary Zone is selected and that Store The Zone In Active Directory is selected. Click Next.

5. On the Active Directory Zone Replication Scope page, ensure that To All DNS Servers In The Active Directory Domain Contoso*xx*.local is selected. Click Next.

6. On the Forward Or Reverse Lookup Zones page, ensure that Forward Lookup Zone is selected, and then click Next.

7. In the Zone Name text box, type **Contoso*xx*.com**, and then click Next.

8. On the Dynamic Update page, ensure that Allow Only Secure Dynamic Updates is selected. Click Next.

9. The Completing The New Zone Wizard page should look like the following figure from Computer03. Click Finish.

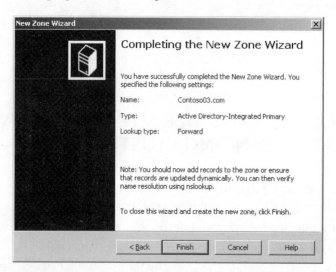

10. In the DNS console, under Computer*yy*, expand Forward Lookup Zones, select and then right-click Contoso*xx*.com, and then select New Host (A).

11. In the New Host dialog box, in the Name text box, type **www**. In the IP Address text box, type **192.168.0.1*xx***, and then click Add Host. Click OK, and then click Done.

12. The DNS Management console should now display a new host (A) record, as shown in the following figure from Computer03. Close the DNS Management console.

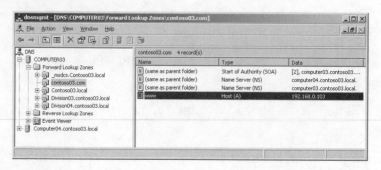

Accessing the Web Site Using the Network Load Balancing Cluster

Now that you have updated DNS, you can access the Web site using its FQDN according to the following steps.

> **IMPORTANT**   *Complete the following steps on both computers.*

1. From the Start menu, point to All Programs, and then select Internet Explorer.

2. In Internet Explorer, in the Address text box, type **http://www .contosoxx.com**, and then press ENTER. (You might be asked for credentials; if so, use your Administrator credentials.)

   > **NOTE**   *If you do not see a Web page referencing the Contoso Web site at this point, you may need to copy the Default.htm file from C:\Lab Manual \Lab09 to the C:\Inetpub\wwwroot folder on your computer (as discussed in the Before You Begin section of this lab).*

3. A Web site with the words "This is an example website for Contoso" should appear.

4. In the Address text box, type **http://192.168.1.1xx**, and then press ENTER. (You might be asked for credentials; if so, use your Administrator credentials.)

   > **QUESTION**   *Why does this second cluster IP address resolve to the Contoso Web site?*

EXERCISE 11-3: OBSERVING AND TROUBLESHOOTING NETWORK LOAD BALANCING CLUSTERS

Estimated completion time: 35 minutes

Now that you have installed a Network Load Balancing cluster, you want to become more familiar with how it works, how it is configured, and how to troubleshoot it.

To do so, you will explore some tools for observing Network Load Balancing. You will also introduce various breaks in the Network Load Balancing cluster and observe the effects using the Nlb command, the Network Load Balancing Manager, and the Event Viewer console.

Using the Nlb Command to View Network Load Balancing Cluster Information on the Local Host

The following steps use the Nlb command to view configuration information of the local implementation of Network Load Balancing.

1. From the Start menu, select Run.

2. In the Run dialog box, in the Open text box, type **cmd**, and then press ENTER.

3. At the command prompt, type **nlb display all**. Information pertaining to Network Load Balancing will be displayed.

> **NOTE** The first set of information, an example of which is relayed in the following sample output (from Computer03), is a report on parameters as they are currently defined in the registry. This might or might not represent the current settings exactly, but rather represents the settings the system would attempt to use if, for example, a reload were to occur (the Nlb Reload command accomplishes this). The second set of information is a set of recent events recorded in the system event log pertaining to Network Load Balancing. You examine events in the event log later in this exercise, and this section of information has been left out of the following sample output.

```
C:\Documents and Settings\Administrator>nlb display all
WLBS Cluster Control Utility V2.4 (c) 1997-2003 Microsoft Corporation.
Cluster 192.168.0.103

=== Configuration: ===

Current time             = 7/15/2004 11:40:26 PM
ParametersVersion        = 4
VirtualNICName           =
AliveMsgPeriod           = 1000
AliveMsgTolerance        = 5
NumActions               = 100
NumPackets               = 200
NumAliveMsgs             = 66
ClusterNetworkAddress    = 02-bf-c0-a8-00-67
ClusterName              = www.Contoso03.com
ClusterIPAddress         = 192.168.0.103
ClusterNetworkMask       = 255.255.255.0
DedicatedIPAddress       = 192.168.0.3
DedicatedNetworkMask     = 255.255.255.0
HostPriority             = 1
ClusterModeOnStart       = STARTED
PersistedStates          = NONE
DescriptorsPerAlloc      = 512
MaxDescriptorAllocs      = 512
TCPConnectionTimeout     = 60
IPSecConnectionTimeout   = 86400
FilterICMP               = DISABLED
ScaleSingleClient        = 0
NBTSupportEnable         = 1
```

```
MulticastSupportEnable    = 0
MulticastARPEnable        = 1
MaskSourceMAC             = 1
IGMPSupport               = DISABLED
IPtoMcastIP               = ENABLED
McastIPAddress            = 0.0.0.0
NetmonAliveMsgs           = 0
EffectiveVersion          = V2.1
IPChangeDelay             = 60000
IPToMACEnable             = 1
ConnectionCleanupDelay    = 300000
RemoteControlEnabled      = 0
RemoteControlUDPPort      = 2504
RemoteControlCode         = 0x0
RemoteMaintenanceEnabled  = 0x0
CurrentVersion            = V2.4
InstallDate               = 0x40F776F8
VerifyDate                = 0x0
NumberOfRules             = 1
BDATeaming                = DISABLED
TeamID                    =
Master                    = DISABLED
ReverseHash               = DISABLED
IdentityHeartbeatPeriod   = 10000
IdentityHeartbeatEnabled  = ENABLED
PortRules
Virtual IP addr Start   End    Prot   Mode      Pri   Load    Affinity

                ALL  80    80    Both   Multiple        Equal   S
```

QUESTION All network adapters have a unique MAC address, comprising six hexadecimal numbers (a 48-bit number capable of representing 2^48 NICs, but some bits are reserved for things like manufacturer serial numbers). ARP resolves IP addresses to MAC addresses. From the output you received using the Nlb Display All command, on both your computer and your partner's computer, what can you say about the ClusterNetworkAddress parameter?

QUESTION The fact that the MulticastSupportEnable parameter is set to 0 indicates the type of operation mode that the cluster is using. What is the operation mode?

QUESTION There are parameters called IdentityHeartbeatPeriod and IdentityHeartbeatEnabled. What is an identity heartbeat in Network Load Balancing?

QUESTION In what percentage is the load distributed among the hosts in your cluster?

4. Open the Network Connections window, or restore it if it is already open.

5. In the Network Connections dialog box, double-click the Cluster network connection.

6. In the taskbar, double-click the time display. Arrange the Cluster Status dialog box and the Date And Time Properties dialog box so that you can view both simultaneously.

7. Note the Packets field in the Cluster Status window is incrementing. Using the clock, count how much it increases over a period of 10 seconds.

> **QUESTION** Assuming that this traffic is caused by the identity heartbeat (it is), and assuming that you counted about 10 heartbeats in 10 seconds (the identity heartbeat is issued once per second), what unit of measure is used for the IdentityHeartbeatPeriod parameter in the preceding sample output? (Recall that it read IdentityHeartbeatPeriod = 10000.)

8. Close the Date And Time Properties dialog box after noting what time it is for use in the next exercise.

Observing the Effects of Disabling a Cluster Network Connection

The following steps disable a network connection bound to Network Load Balancing and then enable you to observe the effects.

> **IMPORTANT** Complete the following steps on the even-numbered computer.

1. In the Cluster Status dialog box, click Disable.

2. At a command prompt, type **nlb display all**.

> **QUESTION** What does running the Nlb Display All command tell you about what occurs when a network connection bound to Network Load Balancing is disabled?

3. In the Network Load Balancing Manager console, select and then right-click www.Contoso.com (192.168.0.1xx), and then select Refresh. An example of the results from Computer04 is shown in the following figure.

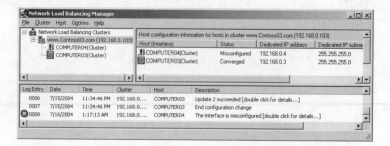

4. Double-click the last event in the log pane. Once you have read it, click OK.

   QUESTION What are the two issues in the log entry?

5. From the Start menu, point to Administrative Tools, and then select Event Viewer.

6. In the Event Viewer console, in the scope pane, select System.

7. In the details pane, search for an event that has a source of WLBS. Ideally, assuming you completed step 1 of this task shortly after completing the preceding task, "Using the Nlb Command to View Network Load Balancing Cluster Information on the Local Host," find an event that occurred just after the time you noted previously (it should be the most recent event logged with a source of WLBS). Double-click the event. Read the event, and then click OK.

   NOTE The System log more accurately reports the Cluster mode as stopped, rather than WLBS as not installed (which is what the Nlb Display All command reported).

8. In the Network Connections window, right-click Cluster, and then select Enable.

9. In the Network Load Balancing Manager console, select and then right-click www.Contoso.com (192.168.0.1xx), and then select Refresh. The warning tag should be removed from the COMPUTERyy node in the scope pane.

10. Close any open windows except the command prompt window, Network Connections, and the Network Load Balancing Manager console.

Interrupting Connectivity to a Network Connection Bound to a Network Load Balancing Cluster

You have had great success with the new Network Load Balancing cluster that is hosting the company's Web site. However, the cluster fails, and you must use several tools, including the Network Load Balancing Manager console and the Nlb command, to analyze what has happened.

   IMPORTANT Complete the following steps on both computers.

1. Disconnect the crossover cable from your Cluster NIC (this needs to be done on only one computer in your pair).

2. In the Network Load Balancing Manager console, select and then right-click www.Contoso.com (192.168.0.1*xx*), and then select Refresh.

> **QUESTION**   According to information in the details pane, what is the status of both hosts in the cluster?

3. At the command prompt, type **nlb params**, and then press ENTER.

4. At the command prompt, type **nlb query**, and then press ENTER.

> **QUESTION**   What does the Nlb Query command reveal about your cluster?

5. Reconnect the crossover cable between the two cluster network adapters.

Network Load Balancing and Media Access Control Addresses

To better understand the relationship between the virtual IP addresses used by clusters and MAC addresses complete the following steps.

1. At the command prompt, type **nlb ip2mac 192.168.0.1*xx***, and then press ENTER.

2. At the command prompt, type **ipconfig /all**, and then press ENTER. The following text contains sample output from these two commands from Computer03.

```
C:\Documents and Settings\Administrator>nlb ip2mac 192.168.0.103
WLBS Cluster Control Utility V2.4 (c) 1997-2003 Microsoft Corporation.
Cluster:           192.168.0.103
Unicast MAC:       02-bf-c0-a8-00-67
Multicast MAC:     03-bf-c0-a8-00-67
IGMP Multicast MAC: 01-00-5e-7f-00-67

C:\Documents and Settings\Administrator>ipconfig /all

Windows IP Configuration

    Host Name . . . . . . . . . . . : computer03
    Primary Dns Suffix  . . . . . . : Contoso03.local
    Node Type . . . . . . . . . . . : Unknown
    IP Routing Enabled. . . . . . . : Yes
    WINS Proxy Enabled. . . . . . . : No
    DNS Suffix Search List. . . . . : Contoso03.local

Ethernet adapter Local Area Connection:

    Connection-specific DNS Suffix  . :
    Description . . . . . . . . . . . : Realtek RTL8139 Family PCI Fast
```

```
Ethernet
NIC #2
    Physical Address. . . . . . . . . : 00-E0-4C-ED-EE-C6
    DHCP Enabled. . . . . . . . . . : No
    IP Address. . . . . . . . . . . : 10.1.1.3
    Subnet Mask . . . . . . . . . . : 255.255.255.0
    Default Gateway . . . . . . . . :
    DNS Servers . . . . . . . . . . : 10.1.1.3

Ethernet adapter Cluster:

    Connection-specific DNS Suffix  . :
    Description . . . . . . . . . . : Realtek RTL8139 Family PCI Fast
Ethernet
NIC
    Physical Address. . . . . . . . . : 02-BF-C0-A8-00-67
    DHCP Enabled. . . . . . . . . . : No
    IP Address. . . . . . . . . . . : 192.168.1.103
    Subnet Mask . . . . . . . . . . : 255.255.255.0
    IP Address. . . . . . . . . . . : 192.168.0.103
    Subnet Mask . . . . . . . . . . : 255.255.255.0
    IP Address. . . . . . . . . . . : 192.168.0.3
    Subnet Mask . . . . . . . . . . : 255.255.255.0
    Default Gateway . . . . . . . . :
    DNS Servers . . . . . . . . . . : 10.1.1.3
```

QUESTION   Is the MAC address for the unicast mode different from the actual MAC of the NIC? Explain why.

LAB CLEANUP

Estimated completion time: 5 minutes

The following steps remove your computer from the cluster and disable the Cluster network adapter. The Lab Cleanup must be completed before continuing to Lab Challenge 11-1 or any future labs.

1. In the Network Load Balancing Clusters Manager console, in the scope pane, select www.Contoso03.com (192.168.0.1*xx*), and then from the Cluster menu, select Delete.

2. Click Yes when prompted to remove Network Load Balancing from all the hosts that are members of the selected cluster.

3. Wait until step 2 completes, and then close the Network Load Balancing Manager console.

4. In the Network Connections window, right-click Cluster, and then select Disable.

5. Close any open windows.

LAB REVIEW QUESTIONS

Estimated completion time: 15 minutes

1. You recently replaced a single host Web server that hosts the Contoso.com Web site with a Network Load Balancing cluster, and now clients are unable to reach Web sites on the server. Preliminary testing suggests the problem has to do with DNS. What it the most likely problem and how can it be fixed?

2. The Nlb Display command solicits its information from the registry, which might not represent the current Network Load Balancing configuration. Which Nlb command supplies the same configuration information, but queries the kernel-mode driver for Network Load Balancing and so receives up-to-date information?

3. You want to install a cluster to increase the reliability of a news server that is updated multiple times each minute by Internet news sources. What type of cluster should you use?

4. Judging by the number of unique identifiers (priority numbers) available to nodes in your Network Load Balancing cluster, how many nodes can a Network Load Balancing cluster contain, assuming all nodes are running Microsoft Windows Server 2003, Enterprise Edition?

5. To improve the performance and reliability of the Contoso network, you add another two computers to the two-computer cluster. Is this an example of scaling up or scaling out?

LAB CHALLENGE 11-1: CONFIGURING A LOCAL QUORUM SERVER CLUSTER

Estimated completion time: 30 minutes

The Network Load Balancing cluster that you have created for the Contoso Web site works well because the data on it is relatively stateless; that is, it changes infrequently. For stateful applications, in which the data changes frequently, Network Load Balancing clusters are impractical because each host maintains its own store of the data used by applications for which the hosts are clustered.

To provide better failover capabilities to Contoso's e-mail servers, you need to implement a different type of cluster: a server cluster. However, because a true server cluster requires a storage area network (SAN), usually based on Fibre Channel or Small Computer System Interface (SCSI), and you don't have one at your disposal, you are going to configure a lone-wolf (contains a local quorum of one) server cluster to become familiar with it.

To complete this lab challenge:

- Install a server cluster using an IP address of 10.1.1.2*xx*.

- Ping the virtual IP address of the cluster to ensure that it works.

- Browse the console tree of the Cluster Administrator console and answer the following questions.

> **QUESTION**   What is the quorum resource, and what does it tell you about the server cluster?

> **QUESTION**   How can you stop the Cluster service through the Cluster Administrator console?

Once you have answered the preceding questions, stop the Cluster service.

SYSTEM ADMINISTRATION AND TERMINAL SERVICES

This lab contains the following exercises and activities:

- Exercise 12-1: Customizing and Using the Microsoft Management Console for Remote Access

- Exercise 12-2: Using HTML Remote Administration Tools

- Exercise 12-3: Using Remote Desktop For Administration

- Exercise 12-4: Issuing and Accepting Remote Assistance Invitations Using a File

- Lab Cleanup

- Lab Review Questions

- Lab Challenge 12-1: Using Group Policy to Configure Remote Desktop

- Lab Challenge 12-2: Configuring a Terminal Server

SCENARIO

You are a network administrator for Contoso, Ltd. The domain controllers and many of the servers at Contoso are isolated in secure rooms with strong air conditioning to keep the servers cool. Because of this, you cannot access them directly except on rare occasions when it is absolutely necessary.

Therefore, to work remotely on the servers, you need to configure several tools. Among them are the MMC, Remote Desktop For Administration, and HTML Remote Administration tools.

Additionally, rather than install separate copies of certain applications on all computers at the call centers at Contoso, you have elected to create some terminal servers.

> **IMPORTANT** You might receive security warnings during this lab issued by Microsoft Internet Explorer. Add any Web sites used to your list of trusted sites, and choose not to display future warnings when asked.

After completing this lab, you will be able to:

- Customize the Microsoft Management Console (MMC) and use it for remote administration.
- Use HTML Remote Administration tools
- Use Remote Desktop For Administration
- Issue and accept invitations for Remote Assistance
- Configure a terminal server

Estimated completion time: 95 minutes

BEFORE YOU BEGIN

To complete the lab challenges, you must ensure that the following dependencies are completed.

- You must install the Group Policy Management Console (GPMC) using the Gpmc.msi installer package, if you did not do so in the Lab Challenge 4-1 for Lab 4, "Group Policy Strategy," or the Before You Begin section in Lab 5, "Software Deployment and Restrictions Using Group Policy," or Lab 6, "Microsoft Windows Server 2003 Security Configuration." To install GPMC, run Gpmc.msi, which is located in the C:\Lab Manual\Lab05 folder, and follow the on-screen instructions.

- If you did not do so in the Before You Begin section of Lab 5 or Lab 6, you must run the ADUCUpdate*xx*.vbs file located in C:\Lab Manual\Lab05. This script creates the structure pictured in Figure 12-1.

This lab often refers to the number of your domain, your computer, and your partner's computer according to the following conventions:

- *xx* is the number of your domain.
- *yy* is the number of your computer.
- *zz* is the number of your partner's computer.

For example, if you are using Computer04, *xx* = 03 (you are a member of Contoso03.local), *yy* = 04 (you are using Computer04), and *zz* = 03 (your partner is using Computer03).

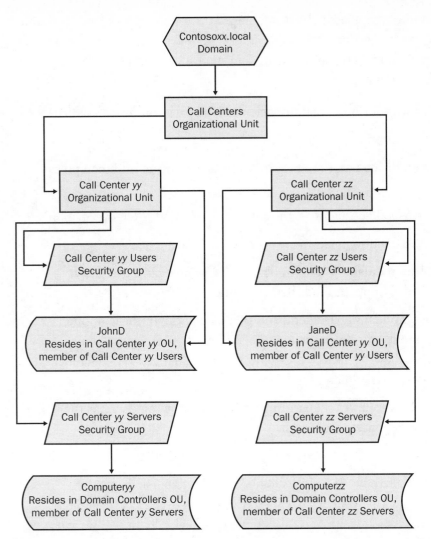

Figure 12-1   Using the ADUCUpdate*xx*.vbs script creates this structure within Active Directory

EXERCISE 12-1: CUSTOMIZING AND USING THE MICROSOFT MANAGEMENT CONSOLE FOR REMOTE ACCESS

Estimated completion time: 15 minutes

Contoso has recently hired a new group of network administrators that will need to be able to perform several tasks on remote computers on the network.

The easiest way for them to be able to perform these tasks is by using a Microsoft Management Console (MMC) with functionality limited to the tasks that they will be asked to perform on a daily basis.

You need to create this MMC for them. It should enable them to administer user and computer accounts in the domain, manage remote computers, and view events on remote computers to be better able to troubleshoot problems. It should also remove the extensions responsible for several tasks they will not need to perform. Finally, it should change to which computer it connects to according to a command-line parameter.

1. Log on with your Administrator account (the password is **P@ssw0rd**).

2. From the Start menu, select Run.

3. In the Run dialog box, in the Open text box, type **mmc**, and then press ENTER.

4. In the Console1 console, from the File menu, select Add/Remove Snap-In.

5. In the Add/Remove Snap-In dialog box, click Add.

6. In the Add Standalone Snap-In dialog box, select Active Directory Users And Computers, and then click Add.

7. Select Computer Management, and then click Add. In the Computer Management console, in the Snap-In Will Always Manage section, select the Allow The Selected Computer To Be Changed When Launching From The Command Line check box. Click Finish.

8. Add the Event Viewer snap-in, and configure it the same way as the Computer Management snap-in.

9. In the Add Standalone Snap-In dialog box, click Close.

10. In the Add/Remove Snap-In dialog box, in the Extensions tab, in the Snap-Ins That Can Be Extended drop-down list, select Computer Management. Clear the Add All Extensions check box.

11. Clear the Disk Management Extension and the Removable Storage Extension check boxes. The following figure shows the correct configuration. Click OK.

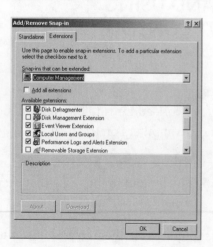

12. In the Console1 console, from the File menu, select Options.

13. In the textbox next to the Change Icon button, type **AdminConsole**. In the Console Mode drop-down list, select each of the options and read the description, and then select User Mode - Full Access. Click OK.

14. In the **AdminConsole** console, from the File menu, select Save As.

15. In the Save As dialog box, save the console to the root of the C drive as AdminConsole (the Administrative Tools folder is the default location).

> **TIP** Normally, you would not save an MMC console in the root; you are doing so here as a convenience for when you use the command line some steps hence. In the real world, you might save an MMC to a shared location to which you have access from different computers on the network or in a location on your computer that is specified in the path so that specifying the location is not necessary when launching it from the Run dialog box or the command line.

16. Close the AdminConsole.

17. Open a Run dialog box.

18. In the Run dialog box, in the Open text box, type **mmc /computer= computerzz C:\AdminConsole.msc**.

> **QUESTION** To which computer are the three snap-ins connected?

19. Having examined the snap-ins, you realize that the Disk Defragmenter option cannot be used on remote computers, and so you want to remove it from the snap-in.

> **QUESTION** Why can't you remove it now by accessing Add/Remove Snap-Ins from the File menu?

20. Close the Admin console.

21. Open a Run dialog box. In the Open text box, type **mmc /a C:\AdminConsole.msc**, and then press ENTER.

> **QUESTION** What does the /a parameter do in the Mmc command?

22. In the AdminConsole console, from the File menu, select Add/Remove Snap-In.

23. In the Add/Remove Snap-In dialog box, in the Extensions tab, in the Snap-Ins That Can Be Extended drop-down list, select Computer Management.

24. In the Available Extensions list box, clear the Disk Defragmenter check box, and then click OK.

25. Close the AdminConsole console, and save the changes when prompted by the Microsoft Management Console message box.

EXERCISE 12-2: USING HTML REMOTE ADMINISTRATION TOOLS

Estimated completion time: 25 minutes

You spend a great deal of time away from your desk and would like to be able to complete some configuration tasks on the servers from your Pocket PC. To do this, you are going to install HTML Remote Administration tools. This will enable you to access a Web page that allows administration over a subset of server functionality.

Installing HTML Remote Administration Tools

The following steps install HTML Remote Administration tools.

1. From the Start menu, point to Control Panel, and then select Add Or Remove Programs.

2. In the Add Or Remove Programs dialog box, click the Add/Remove Windows Components icon on the left.

3. In the Windows Components Wizard, on the Windows Components page, select Application Server, and then click Details.

4. In the Application Server dialog box, select Internet Information Services, and then click Details.

5. In the Internet Information Services dialog box, select World Wide Web Service, and then click Details.

6. In the World Wide Web Service dialog box, select the Remote Administration (HTML) check box. Click OK.

7. In the Internet Information Services dialog box, click OK.

8. In the Application Server dialog box, click OK.

9. In the Windows Components Wizard, on the Windows Components page, click Next.

10. The Configuring Components page will appear and indicate installation progress.

11. On the Completing The Windows Components Wizard page, click Finish.

12. Close the Add Or Remove Programs dialog box.

Connecting to a Server Running the HTML Remote Administration Service

The following steps connect to your partner's computer's HTML Administration Web site.

> **IMPORTANT** Wait until your partner has completed the previous task before continuing.

1. From the Start menu, point to All Programs, and then select Internet Explorer.

2. In Internet Explorer, in the Address text box, type **https://computerzz:8098**, and then press ENTER.

> **QUESTION** What does the s appended to http signify in the address?

3. In the Security Alert message box, click Yes to accept the untrusted certificate and proceed.

4. In the Connect To Computer03 dialog box, enter your Administrator credentials.

5. In the Internet Explorer message pertaining to security, click Add to add the site to your list of trusted sites.

6. In the Trusted Sites dialog box, click Add, and then click Close.

7. In a moment, the Welcome page of the HTML Remote Administration
    Web site will appear, as shown in the following figure from Computer04.

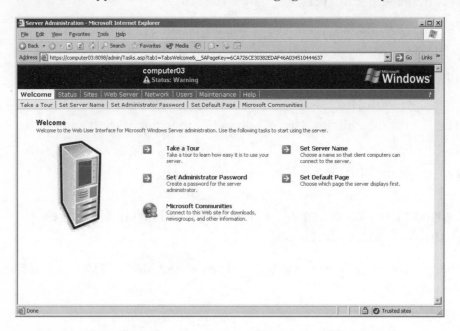

Configuring the HTML Administration Access IP Address

To increase the security of the Server Administration Web site, you want to
configure it to be served only over a single network adapter. This network
adapter has only internal connectivity, and therefore the site will not be able to
be breached by outside sources.

1. Click Network in the navigation frame at the top of the Web site.

2. On the Network page, click Administration Web Site.

3. On the Administration Web Site Properties page, select Just This IP
    Address. Ensure that 10.1.1.zz is selected in the Just This IP Address
    drop-down list (it should be the only option available).

4. Click OK.

5. In the Security Alert message box, click Yes to proceed.

6. In the Connect To 10.1.1.zz dialog box, enter your Administrator
    credentials, and then click OK.

7. In the Internet Explorer message box, add the site to your trusted sites
    list using the same technique you used earlier in this exercise.

8. On the Remote Administration Tools page, click the link back to the
    default home page.

> **NOTE** If you do not receive a session expired message or see a link to the default home page, you will probably be looking at the Network page. If this happens, click the tab to return to the Server Administration page.

Starting a Remote Desktop Session Using the Server Administration Web Page

The functionality of using the HTML Server Administration Web site is limited. To gain full control of a remote server, you want to be able to take over the desktop. The following steps enable you to do just that.

1. From the Start menu, right-click My Computer, and then select Properties.

2. In the System Properties dialog box, in the Remote tab, in the Remote Desktop section, select the Allow Users To Connect Remotely To This Computer check box. Click OK.

> **NOTE** Ensure your partner has completed steps 1 and 2 before continuing.

3. On the Server Administration Web site, click the Maintenance link in the navigation bar.

4. On the Maintenance page, click Remote Desktop.

5. In the Security Warning message box, click Yes to accept the ActiveX Control installation.

6. In the Log On To Windows dialog box, enter your Administrator credentials, and then click OK. You have now logged on to your partner's computer, and you are looking at your partner's desktop.

7. Close the shared desktop window.

8. Close Internet Explorer.

EXERCISE 12-3: USING REMOTE DESKTOP FOR ADMINISTRATION

Estimated completion time: 20 minutes

The most easy and complete way of controlling a remote server is by using Remote Desktop For Administration.

To be able to administer Contoso's domain controllers fully from the comforts of your cubicle, you need to configure Remote Desktop For Administration. Later in the exercise, you will tighten up security.

Allowing Remote Assistance and Remote Desktop

The following steps enable your computer to be both a client and server of Remote Desktop.

1. From the Start menu, right-click My Computer, and then select Properties.

2. In the System Properties dialog box, in the Remote tab, select the Turn On Remote Assistance And Allow Invitations To Be Sent From This Computer check box. Ensure that the Allow Users To Connect Remotely To This Computer check box remains selected.

3. In the Remote Sessions message box, click OK.

4. Click Advanced.

5. In the Remote Assistant Settings dialog box, in the Invitations Section, in the drop-down list, verify that 30 is selected, and select Minutes. Click OK.

> **QUESTION**   What does clearing the Allow This Computer To Be Controlled Remotely check box in the Remote Assistant Settings dialog box (from the previous step) cause to happen?

6. In the System Properties dialog box, click OK.

> **IMPORTANT**   When you and your partner have both completed this task, you can complete the last task of the previous exercise.

Using the Remote Desktop Connection Dialog Box

The following steps use the Remote Desktop Connection dialog box to connect to your partner's domain controller.

1. From the Start menu, point to All Programs, Accessories, Communications, and then select Remote Desktop Connection.

2. In the Remote Desktop Connection dialog box, click Options. This causes the Remote Desktop Connection dialog box to appear as shown in the following figure.

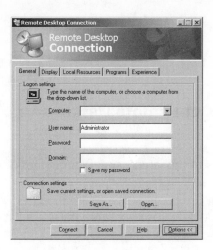

3. Open the Display tab.

> **QUESTION**   What is different about Microsoft Windows 2000 Server
> Terminal Services in Remote Administration mode compared to Microsoft
> Windows Server 2003 Remote Desktop For Administration that is
> revealed in the Colors section of this tab?

4. In the Experience tab, clear the Bitmap Caching check box, and check
   the remainder of the check boxes. The configuration should be as
   shown in the following figure.

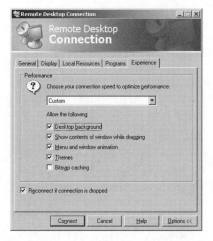

5. Return to the General tab. In the Computer text box, type **Computerzz**,
   and enter your Administrator credentials. Once your partner has
   completed this step, you should be looking at your partner's desktop,
   and your partner should be looking at yours.

6. Close the Remote Desktop session by clicking the Close button on the control bar at the top of your screen.

7. In the Disconnect Windows Session message box, click OK.

Modifying Server-Side Settings of Remote Desktop For Administration

To tighten the security of servers that are administered using Remote Desktop, you need to complete the following:

■ Restrict users to one session (which avoids misconfiguration).

■ Use High encryption.

■ Always ask for a password at logon.

■ End disconnected sessions after 5 minutes and idle connections after 10 minutes (which prevents hackers from finding and using a Remote Desktop client that was accidentally left connected).

■ Allow only one connection at a time.

The following steps configure the stated security settings:

1. From the Start menu, point to Administrative Tools, and then select Terminal Services Configuration.

2. In the Terminal Services Configuration manager, in the scope pane, select Server Settings.

> **QUESTION**   When temporary files are created in a Remote Desktop session, are the temporary folders and files deleted at the end of the session by default?

3. Double-click Restrict Each User To One Session. In the Single Session Per User dialog box, select the Restrict Each User To One Session dialog box, and then click OK.

4. In the scope pane, select Connections. In the details pane, right-click RDP-tcp, and then select Properties.

5. In the RDP-tcp Properties dialog box, in the Encryption Level drop-down list, select High.

6. In the Logon Settings tab, select the Always Prompt For Password check box.

7. On the Sessions page, select both Override Users Settings check boxes.

8. In the End A Disconnected Session drop-down list, select 5 Minutes. Leave the Active Session Limit at Never, and set the Idle Session Limit to 10 Minutes. These settings are shown configured correctly in the following figure.

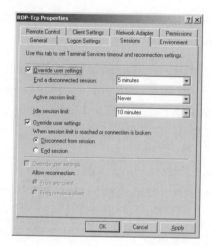

9. In the Network Adapter tab, in the Maximum Connections numeral box, select 1, and then click OK.

10. Close the Terminal Services Configuration console.

> **IMPORTANT** Wait until your partner has completed step 10 before continuing.

11. Access the Remote Desktop Connection dialog box, and click Options if they are not displayed already. Ensure that Computerzz is displayed in the Computer selection box.

12. In the General tab, enter your Administrator credentials, and then click Connect.

> **NOTE** Note that on the remote server you are again queried for your password, as specified in the RDP-tcp settings.

13. Click Cancel in the Log On To Windows dialog box. Close the Remote Desktop Connection dialog box.

> **NOTE** If you have time, you might want to test some of these settings. For example, wait 10 minutes while remaining idle to see whether your session disconnects, and see how many remote desktop sessions you can create with your partner.

EXERCISE 12-4: ISSUING AND ACCEPTING REMOTE ASSISTANCE INVITATIONS USING A FILE

Estimated completion time: 15 minutes

Some users need assistance frequently. Currently, you have been walking to their computers (often in different buildings) and fixing the problems on site.

You have decided to implement Remote Assistance so that these users can ask for help. You will create a shared folder in which the users can deposit an invitation. A desktop technician can then call the user, get a password, and help the user using Remote Desktop.

> **TIP**   Many technicians that use Remote Assistance find that it is often easier to offer an invitation to the person that needs help rather than have the person create an invitation asking for help. To enable offering Remote Assistance for the Administrators group, access the Remote Assistance node in Group Policy (the location of this is covered in Lab Challenge 12-1, "Using Group Policy to Configure Remote Desktop"), and, in the details pane, double-click Offer Remote Assistance, select Enabled, and then click OK.

> **IMPORTANT**   Complete the following steps on the odd-numbered computer only.

1. Ensure that the desktop has the focus, and then press F1.

2. In the Help And Support Center dialog box, under Support Tasks, click Tools.

3. On the Tools page, in the navigation pane, expand Help And Support Tools, and then select Remote Assistance.

4. On the Remote Assistance page, click Invite Someone To Help You.

5. After the Loading message disappears, click Save Invitation As A File (Advanced) at the bottom of the page.

6. On the Remote Assistance - Save Invitation page, accept the defaults, and then click Continue.

7. In the Microsoft Internet Explorer message box, click OK to continue.

> **QUESTION**   Why does this message box appear?

8. Click Continue.

9. In the Type Password and Confirm Password text boxes, type **P@ssw0rd2**. Click Save Invitation.

> **TIP** When creating a password, ensure that the password is conveyed through a different medium than the invitation (for example, by phone). This way, if an invitation is intercepted, security will not be breached unless the password is intercepted independently.

10. In the Save As dialog box, save the Invitation with the default file name (RAInvitation.msrcincident) to a shared folder named Share that your partner can access, and go to step 16. If such a folder does not exist, follow steps 11 through 15 to create one first, and then save the file to it.

11. In the Save As dialog box, navigate to C:\, and then click the New Folder icon at the top.

12. For the name of the new folder, type **Share**.

13. Right-click the Share folder, and then select Sharing And Security.

14. In the Share Properties dialog box, select Share This Folder, and then click OK.

15. Save the file to the Share folder with the default file name.

16. Close the Help And Support Center.

> **IMPORTANT** Complete the following steps on the even-numbered computer.

17. Open the RAInvitation.msrcincident file that your partner just saved to the shared folder. (To access the share, open a Run dialog box, in the Open text box type **computerzz\share**, and then press ENTER.)

18. In the Remote Assistance dialog box, in the Password text box, type **P@ssw0rd2**, and then click Yes. A Remote Assistance message will appear on the odd-numbered computer.

> **IMPORTANT** Complete the following steps on the odd-numbered computer.

19. In the Remote Assistance dialog box, click Yes.

20. In the Remote Assistance window, in the Message Entry box, type **I need help**, or some other message, and click Send. An example of the Remote Assistance window from the client side is shown in the following figure.

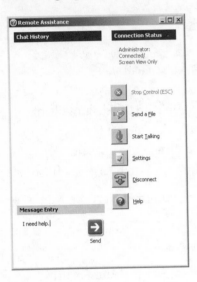

IMPORTANT   Complete the following step on the even-numbered computer.

21. In the Remote Assistance window, click Take Control in the toolbar at the top of the window.

IMPORTANT   Complete the following step on the odd-numbered computer.

22. In the Remote Assistance – Web Page Dialog dialog box, click Yes.

IMPORTANT   Complete the following steps on both computers.

23. On the even-numbered computer, in the Remote Assistance – Web Page Dialog dialog box, click OK. You now have control over your partner's computer. Test this a little, but don't do anything destructive. Click Disconnect.

24. Close the Remote Assistance window on both computers.

LAB CLEANUP

Estimated completion time: 5 minutes

The following must be completed before Lab Challenge 12-1 can be completed. However, if you are not going to complete that lab challenge, there is no need to complete this cleanup.

1. From the Start menu, right-click My Computer, and then select Properties.

2. In the System Properties dialog box, in the Remote tab, clear Turn On Remote Assistance And Allow Invitations To Be Sent From This Computer check box, and clear the Allow Users To Connect Remotely To This Computer check box. Click OK.

3. Close the System Properties dialog box.

LAB REVIEW QUESTIONS

Estimated completion time: 15 minutes

1. What four console modes are available in an MMC console?

2. In Exercise 12-3, "Using Remote Desktop For Administration," you used Remote Desktop For Administration, and in Exercise 12-4, "Issuing and Accepting Remote Assistance Invitations Using a File," you used Remote Assistance. Permissions derived from which user account were given to the client accessing the remote computer in each instance?

3. What built-in security group contains users that can log on to a terminal server or that can become a client in a Remote Desktop For Administration session?

4. In Exercise 12-3, you configured Remote Desktop For Administration to use High encryption. How many bits does this security level employ for the corresponding decryption keys, and what is the drawback of using this higher security?

5. Invitations for Remote Assistance can employ an extra level of security when the invitation is created. How is this security provided, and how should it be implemented for best results?

LAB CHALLENGE 12-1: USING GROUP POLICY TO CONFIGURE REMOTE DESKTOP

Estimated completion time: 15 minutes

You want to enable all member computers of a specific organizational unit (OU) to request Remote Assistance. However, you do not want to make the required changes on each computer individually.

> **NOTE** Because the only OU populated with computers in the lab is the DC OU, it is used as an example. In the real world, it is much more likely that the OU would be populated with workstations running Microsoft Windows XP Professional.

You need to use Group Policy to create a policy for domain controllers that configures Remote Desktop For Administration. To complete this challenge, modify domain controller Group Policy to do the following:

- Configure the domain controllers to be Remote Desktop clients
- Ensure that the client settings enable the computer to be remotely controlled
- Allow a maximum ticket value of 10 minutes
- Update Group Policy and ensure by creating a file invitation that the policy has been updated

LAB CHALLENGE 12-2: CONFIGURING A TERMINAL SERVER

Estimated completion time: 30 minutes

Rather than install individual copies of certain applications on the thin clients of the Call Center yy OU, you have decided to set up a terminal server that will serve these applications (it is not a best practice to set up a domain controller as a terminal server, but as an example this lab challenge has you do so).

To complete this lab challenge, you must accomplish the following goals:

- Install Terminal Services on both computers using the Configure Your Server Wizard.
- Define members of the Call Center yy security group as Terminal Services users on both computers.
- Log on as JohnD, if your computer is odd, and JaneD, if your computer is even, to your partner's terminal server.

LAB 13
DISASTER RECOVERY

This lab contains the following exercises and activities:

- Exercise 13-1: Backing Up the System State and Other Items

- Exercise 13-2: Authoritatively Restoring an Active Directory Subtree and Confirming the Restore

- Exercise 13-3: Using the Volume Shadow Copy Service

- Lab Review Questions

- Lab Challenge 13-1: Installing and Starting the Recovery Console

- Lab Challenge 13-2: Creating an ASR Recovery Set

SCENARIO

Contoso requires that all its servers maintain current backups, so that if a disaster ever strikes, the server technicians can quickly restore valid data to the old servers or to new servers with similar hardware.

To accomplish this, server technicians must be familiar with the Backup utility and normal and differential backups. Contoso uses both these backup modes in its backup scheme.

Also, Contoso wants to proactively install local copies of the Recovery Console on servers so that in an emergency the Microsoft Windows Server 2003 installation CD does not need to be located to start the console.

Finally, in case a server must be remade from scratch, you must create an Automated System Recovery (ASR) recovery set.

After completing this lab, you will be able to:

- Back up critical data
- Back up and restore the System State, normally and authoritatively
- Use shadow copies
- Install and access the Recovery Console
- Create an ASR recovery set

Estimated completion time: 90 minutes

BEFORE YOU BEGIN

To complete this lab, you must ensure that the following dependencies are completed.

- The directions in Exercise 13-2 assume that the Group Policy Management Console is installed for use in managing an OU. If the GPMC is not installed, the OU management tasks may be completed using the Active Directory Users And Computers console. To install GPMC, run Gpmc.msi, which is located in the C:\Lab Manual\Lab04 folder, and follow the on-screen instructions.

- If you did not run the ADUCUpdate*xx*.vbs script in Labs 5, 6, 7, 10, or 12, you must run the ADUCUpdate*xx*.vbs file located in C:\Lab Manual\Lab05 on one, but not both, of the computers in your odd-even partner pair. This script will create the structure pictured in Figure 13-1.

This lab often refers to the number of your domain and your computer according to the following conventions:

- *xx* is the number of your domain.
- *yy* is the number of your computer.

For example, if you are using Computer04, *xx* = 03 (you are a member of Contoso03.local), and *yy* = 04 (you are using Computer04).

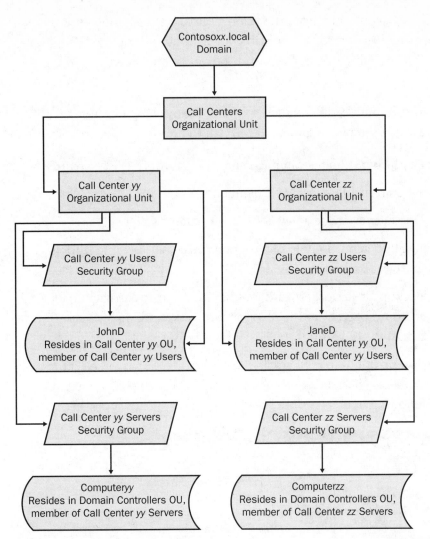

Figure 13-1   Using the ADUCUpdate*xx*.vbs script creates this structure within Active Directory

EXERCISE 13-1: BACKING UP THE SYSTEM STATE AND OTHER ITEMS

Estimated completion time: 30 minutes

Contoso uses the following backup scheme. A normal backup is made of critical data once a week, late at night on Sundays. Each day, a differential backup is created as a file. The file is then copied by an employee from the computer on which it was created onto a removable medium.

By splitting the backup duty from the removable media copy duty, security is increased, because the person responsible for making the copy to the removable media of the backup file has no control over what is contained in the backup file.

You must create a routine, differential backup of the System State along with some critical data used by computers in the Call Center.

1. Log on with your Administrator account (the password is **P@ssw0rd**).

2. From the Start menu, select My Documents.

3. In My Documents, create a new folder and name it **Cache**.

4. From the Start menu, point to All Programs, Accessories, System Tools, and then select Backup.

5. In the Backup Or Restore Wizard, on the Welcome To the Backup Or Restore Wizard page, clear the Always Start In Wizard Mode check box. Click Advanced Mode.

6. In the Backup utility, in the Backup tab, in the directory tree, select the My Documents check box and the System State check box, as shown in the following figure.

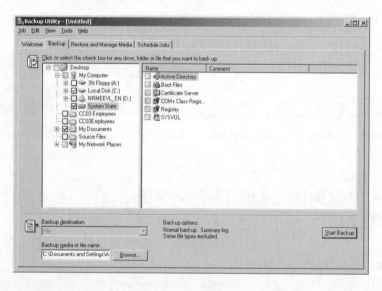

QUESTION   When System State is selected in the directory tree, why are the check boxes in the detail pane unavailable (grayed out)?

7. From the Tools menu, select Options.

8. In the Options dialog box, in the Default Backup Type drop-down list, select Differential.

> **NOTE** You might want to select the other options and read the descriptions, if you are unfamiliar with them.

> **QUESTION** Assume this is the third differential backup of these selections that you have made since the last normal backup. To restore this information to the state of this backup, how many of the four backups (the normal and the three differential) will you have to restore?

> **QUESTION** Given that you have selected Differential backup, what type of backup method will be applied to the System State information?

9. In the Exclude Files tab, under Files Excluded For All Users, click Add New.

10. In the Add Excluded Files dialog box, click Browse.

11. In the Exclude Path dialog box, expand My Documents, and then select the Cache folder. Click OK.

> **NOTE** For the purposes of this lab, pretend that your My Documents folder contains databases used by an application used in the Call Centers called Proseware and that the Cache folder contains cached information that does not need to be backed up.

12. In the Add Excluded Files dialog box, in the Custom File Mask text box, type ***.dat**, and ensure that the Applies To All Subfolders check box is selected. Click OK.

13. In the General tab, ensure that the following check boxes are cleared:

   ❑ Show Alert Message When I Start The Backup Utility And Removable Storage Is Not Running

   ❑ Show Alert Message When I Start The Backup Utility And There Is Recognizable Media Available

   ❑ Show Alert Message When New Media Is Inserted

   ❑ Always Allow Use Of Recognizable Media Without Prompting

> **TIP** These check boxes should be cleared when you are backing up to a file and then copying to another media. They should be selected when you are backing up directly to another media.

14. The General tab should look like the following figure. Click OK.

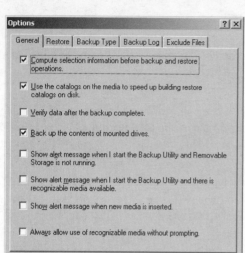

15. In the Backup utility, in the Backup tab, click Start Backup.

> **NOTE** If you receive a Backup Utility message box reporting that drive A is empty, click OK. Click Browse next to the Change The Backup Or Media File Name text box, and specify the My Documents folder as the location to create the Backup.bkf file.

16. In the Backup Job Information dialog box, select Replace The Data On The Media With This Backup option. Click Start Backup.

> **NOTE** If you are presented with a Replace Data message box, click Yes to replace the data (in Lab 8, "Administering Software Update Services," SUS metadata was backed up).

17. The Backup Progress dialog box will appear and indicate progress. This task can take anywhere from 5 minutes to 30 minutes or more.

> **QUESTION** When the backup is under way, you might notice in the Status text box that the message "Preparing to backup using shadow copy" appears. What is shadow copy and why is it being used?

18. When the backup is complete, click Close.

19. Close the Backup utility.

EXERCISE 13-2: AUTHORITATIVELY RESTORING AN ACTIVE DIRECTORY SUBTREE AND CONFIRMING THE RESTORE

Estimated completion time: 35 minutes

You recently told an assistant to "Deplete the Fall, central organizational unit," which is a unit of employees in charge of organizing the Information Technology (IT) department for the fall season. You wanted your assistant to remove some of the members because the unit was too large. But your assistant heard "Delete the Call Centers organizational unit," and did so. This has brought the Call Centers workers to a halt, and you need to take action immediately.

Because you have planned for such disasters, you have a recent backup that contains up-to-date information on the Call Centers organizational unit (OU) for your domain.

You must complete an authoritative restore on the Contoso*xx*.local subtree of the Active Directory directory service. This will restore your Active Directory domain structure while leaving other domains within the same forest alone.

> **IMPORTANT** Complete the following steps on the odd-numbered computer. Do not complete these steps until your partner has finished the previous exercise.

Creating the Problem

The following steps perform the egregious error that your assistant committed.

1. From the Start menu, point to Administrative Tools, and then select Group Policy Management.

2. In the Group Policy Management console, expand Forest: Contoso*xx*.local, expand Domains, expand Contoso*xx*.local, and then select Call Centers.

3. From the Action menu, select Delete.

4. In the Group Policy Management message box, click OK.

5. Force replication to ensure that Active Directory is up-to-date (forcing replication is covered in Exercise 3-4, "Forcing Active Directory Replication to the New DNS Server").

Performing an Authoritative Restore and Confirming the Restore

The following steps restore the desired data in the Directory Services Restore mode, and then confirm the restore by checking Active Directory.

> **IMPORTANT**   Complete the following steps on the even-numbered computer. After replication is forced on the odd-numbered computer, verify that the Call Centers OU was removed from the Active Directory Users And Computers console.

1. Remove any media from your CD/DVD drive or your floppy drive (if your computer is set to boot from removable media, this will make the process of starting Directory Services Restore mode easier).

2. Restart your computer.

3. At the beginning of Windows startup, press F8.

4. On the Windows Advanced Options Menu screen, use the arrow keys to select Directory Services Restore Mode (Windows Domain Controllers Only), and then press ENTER.

5. Log on with your Directory Services Restore mode credentials (these should be the same as your Administrator credentials).

6. In the Desktop message box, click OK to acknowledge that you are running in Safe mode.

7. Open the Backup utility (step 4 in Exercise 13-1).

> **NOTE**   You can also open the Backup utility by typing **ntbackup** and pressing ENTER in the Run dialog box.

8. In the Backup utility, in the Restore And Manage Media tab, in the directory tree, expand File, expand the backup file you created, and select the System State check box, as shown in the following figure.

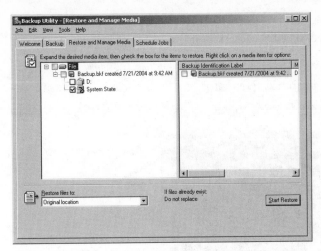

9. Ensure that in the Restore Files To drop-down list that Original Location is selected. Click Start Restore.

10. In the Warning message box, click OK to confirm that the current System State will be overwritten.

11. In the Confirm Restore message box, click OK.

12. The Restore Progress dialog box will appear and indicate progress. This should take about the same amount of time as backing up the data took. When the restore is completed, click Close.

13. When asked by the Backup Utility message box if you want to restart, click No.

14. Close the Backup utility.

15. From the Start menu, select Run.

16. In the Run dialog box, in the Open text box, type **cmd**.

17. At the command prompt, type **ntdsutil**, and press ENTER.

18. At the Ntdsutil prompt, type **authoritative restore**, and then press ENTER.

> **NOTE** When working in this utility, you can abbreviate the words of a command. For example, the above command would have worked if you had typed **a r** instead of typing the full **authoritative restore** command. Try abbreviating the following command, but remember that you need to type at least one letter from each word of the command as well as the complete LDAP path.

19. At the Authoritative Restore prompt, type **restore subtree "OU=Call Centers,DC=Contoso*xx*,DC=local"**, and then press ENTER.

20. In the Authoritative Restore Confirmation Dialog message box, click Yes to perform the authoritative restore on the subtree. The command prompt window should look similar to the following figure.

21. Close the command prompt window.

22. Restart your computer and log on with your Administrator account.

> **IMPORTANT** Complete the following step on both computers.

23. Open the Group Policy Management console, and in the scope pane, expand your domain. Call Centers should be present again (you might need to refresh or wait for or force replication before you see the object on the odd-numbered computer).

EXERCISE 13-3: USING THE VOLUME SHADOW COPY SERVICE

Estimated completion time: 10 minutes

It is quite common for you to be asked by a computer user to restore a file that he or she has accidentally deleted or that has become corrupted. Sometimes you are able to help, and other times you are not.

So that users can be held responsible for restoring files themselves, you are going to activate the Volume Shadow Copy service.

> **IMPORTANT** Complete the following steps on both computers.

Creating a File to Demonstrate Shadow Copy

The following steps create an example file that is deleted later and restored using a shadow copy.

1. If there is not a shared folder named Share on your C drive, create one that your partner has permissions to read and write to.

2. Open the shared folder on your partner's computer.

3. From the File menu, select Text Document.

4. For the name of the text document, type **Test.txt,** and then press ENTER.

Enabling the Volume Shadow Copy Service

The following steps enable the Volume Shadow Copy service and also create an initial shadow copy of all shared folders on the selected volume.

1. From the Start menu, select My Computer.

2. In the My Computer window, right-click Local Disk (C:), and then select Properties.

3. In the Local Disk (C:) Properties dialog box, in the Shadow Copies tab, click Settings.

> **QUESTION**   How many shadow copies are created per day using the default schedule? If you have to open any additional windows to answer this question, be sure to return to the Settings dialog box when you are done.

4. Close the Settings dialog box.

5. In the Local Disk (C:) Properties dialog box, click Enable.

6. In the Enable Shadow Copies dialog box, click Yes. It can take a few minutes for any shared folders on the volume to be copied.

7. Click Create Now.

8. Click OK in the Local Disk (C:) Properties dialog box.

Using Volume Shadow Copy

The following steps delete and then restore the Test.txt file using its shadow copy.

1. Return to the Share folder on your partner's computer (you can connect by opening a Run dialog box, typing **\\Computerzz\Share**, and then pressing ENTER).

2. Delete the Test.txt file.

3. Right-click the folder icon in the upper left of the Share folder, and then select Properties.

> **NOTE** To see the above option, you may need to connect to \\Computerzz instead of \\Computerzz\Share

4. In the Share On 10.1.1.*xx* Properties dialog box, in the Previous Versions tab, select the only version in the Folder Versions list box. Click View.

> **NOTE** Although not installed by default, you can get the Previous Versions Client for Windows XP, Windows 2000, Windows NT 4.0, Windows Me, Windows 98, and Windows 95 operating systems from the Microsoft Web site.

5. Confirm that the Test.txt file is there, and then close the window.

6. In the Share On 10.1.1.*xx* Properties dialog box, click Restore.

7. In the Previous Versions message box, click Yes to confirm that you want to restore the previous version.

8. In the Previous Versions message box, click OK.

9. Close the Share On 10.1.1.*xx* Properties dialog box.

10. Return to the Share folder and confirm that the Test.txt file has been restored. Close the Share folder.

LAB REVIEW QUESTIONS

Estimated completion time: 15 minutes

1. What is backed up when you select the System State for backup?

2. What are the five backup types, and how does each relate to the archive attribute? (Hint: The archive attribute is set to denote a file for backup and can be cleared to mark the file as backed up. Given this information, you can deduce the treatment of the archive attribute for each backup type by reading its description in the Options dialog box in the Backup utility.)

3. In Exercise 13-2, you restored the System State. However, it was only a change to Active Directory that you wanted to restore to an older

version, but you restored the entire System State. Why did you restore all six components of the System State instead of just restoring Active Directory?

4. Exercise 13-2 has you complete an authoritative restore of the System State. How would you modify the procedure so that differences in Active Directory reflected on other domain controllers would be replicated to the restored domain controller so that the restore was normal instead of authoritative?

5. In Exercise 13-3, you enabled shadow copies on the C drive. Why didn't you enable shadow copies just on the shared folders that you wanted to be able to access previous versions of files instead of the entire volume?

LAB CHALLENGE 13-1: INSTALLING AND STARTING THE RECOVERY CONSOLE

Estimated completion time: 15 minutes

In case a server ever goes down to the point that you cannot start it and fix it even in Safe mode, you need to prepare to use the Recovery Console. The Recovery Console can be started by booting from the installation CD and selecting the Repair option, but it can be difficult to track down an installation CD in the labyrinthine catacombs of Contoso.

Therefore, it is recommended that you proactively install the Recovery Console and check to make sure that it works. While you're there, you might as well view the commands available from the console. To complete this lab challenge:

■ Install the Recovery Console.

■ Boot the Recovery Console.

■ List and read the commands that are available.

LAB CHALLENGE 13-2: CREATING AN ASR RECOVERY SET

Estimated completion time: 15 minutes

System recovery can be greatly simplified if you create an Automated System Recovery (ASR) set. This includes a set of backup files and a floppy disk that contains a list of the system files that are installed on the computer. Using these two items, you can easily rebuild a downed server. Although the backup set required is too large to create in a lab environment, you can create and find the files that are copied to the ASR floppy disk.

To complete this lab challenge, start the ASR backup process, cancel it during the backup process, and locate the files that should be copied onto the ASR floppy disk (Hint: Chapter 13, "Disaster Recovery," in the textbook discusses what these files are and where they are located.)